DADDY DAUGHTER

Dynamic
THE PATH TO HEALING

VOLUME I
A COLLABORATIVE WORK
BY THE POWER 13

authorHOUSE®

AuthorHouse™
1663 Liberty Drive
Bloomington, IN 47403
www.authorhouse.com
Phone: 833-262-8899

Published by AuthorHouse 10/13/2022

ISBN: 978-1-6655-7298-9 (sc)
ISBN: 978-1-6655-7297-2 (e)

Library of Congress Control Number: 2022918648

Print information available on the last page.

CONTENTS

A SPECIAL DEDICATION FROM THE POWER 13 CO-AUTHORS

We dedicate our stories to the little girl still inside of us who desired for our daddy to toss us in the air with laughter while we screamed, "Do it again." To all of us who wish we could be a girl, dad in every sense of the phrase. You are enough, and you are lovable.

ADRIENNE CONYERS-BEY: To Pumpkin, Susan, Deja, Yanna, Jayden, and the late Robert Sanders.

DR. LIZ BLANDING: There is a seed of greatness in every adversity. With great adoration, I dedicate my story in this book to the great warrior women "seeds" of my great-grandmother, Hattie Odom.

ROBYN SMITH-HAYNES: To Gabrielle Christian, "Drummer Girl," and Madison Peyton, "Rocky"

SAKINNA J: To the love of my life, George. Thank you for showing our Five daughters the true definition of "a Father's love."

FOCUS JAMES: To all the daughters whose fathers did not have the capacity to father, it was not YOUR fault or YOUR problem to solve.

BEVERLY LARUE: To our heavenly Father, the healer, and restorer of all his daughters with love.

DR. MARLENA SHERMAN LINTON: To James Bates (my grandfather), who planted the seeds, and James Landry Sherman (my father), who waters the seeds that God makes grow.

MAQUIRA OLIVER, LMSW-C: To Junia & Mekelee- My Luvbug, my Best friend/Sister

Also, to that person who keeps me grounded- You encourage me to live my truth.

BRENDA WARREN: To Minnie Lancaster, my mother, for ensuring I walked in forgiveness.

TIFFANY "CRISTENÉ" WASHINGTON, B.S., M.P.S: This work is dedicated to my daughter, Journey Lindan Bell. May God allow you to learn from Mommy's mistakes yet teach from your own experiences. I love you! ♥"

DR. LATISHA WEBB: To two of my – Paternal aunts 'who came for me,' Hattie Crawford and the late Mary Bradford.'

CAPTORIA WILSON: To God and my brother, both constant father figures who taught me how to LOVE!

INTRODUCTION

The Daddy Daughter Dynamic

Is the past the past? Or is it right here in the present, destroying your future? If you don't heal the hurt, you will repeat the pain. Then, you won't be capable of getting the love you want or having the life you love.

In this amazing book, thirteen powerful women share their Daddy Daughter dynamic experiences that have radically changed the trajectory of their lives. The healing part of their journey was just as revolutionary. Read the stories of the Power 13 and see how many of these memoirs resonate with you.

Are you the neglected little girl, the hurting tween, the starving-for-attention teen, the damaged young woman, or the unloved, hurting mature adult? Maybe, you are all the above?

No matter where you find yourself, it's time to draw a line in the sand and begin your healing journey. Here's an eye-opening visual bringing to light many dominating factors in your life, whether you are aware or not. To demonstrate the many parts of our lives affected by the Daddy Daughter relationship, look at this "Wheel of Life". We've added some effects we have experienced in our lives to open your mind to understand WHY now is the time to take care of yourself and heal. Which one of these remnants of your Daddy Daughter Dynamic do you see still controlling life?

The Wheel of Life!

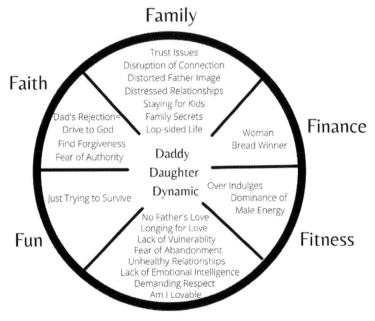

Family

Faith

Finance

Fun

Fitness

Trust Issues
Disruption of Connection
Distorted Father Image
Distressed Relationships
Staying for Kids
Family Secrets
Lop-sided Life

Dad's Rejection=
Drive to God
Find Forgiveness
Fear of Authority

Just Trying to Survive

Daddy
Daughter
Dynamic

Woman
Bread Winner

Over Indulges
Dominance of
Male Energy

No Father's Love
Longing for Love
Lack of Vulnerablity
Fear of Abandonment
Unhealthy Relationships
Lack of Emotional Intelligence
Demanding Respect
Am I Lovable

Love and Deep Intimacy

CHAPTER ONE

From Wounded to Victorious

BY ADRIENNE CONYERS – BEY

My dad was a chef. Cooking is not my favorite thing to do, and I would much rather cook with someone, but when I do cook, I listen to my ancestors for how much seasoning to use and guidance for when the food is done. Maybe my dad contributes to that cooking help in some way. My dad was an artist. I loved to draw as a young girl and teenager. As a young adult, I found myself to be artsy at times.

My mom tells me my dad was musical. Although I love to sing, I took keyboard lessons as a teenager, which was my go-to whenever I was bored or sad. I also sang in a children's and youth choir and my college choir. At some point, I began to sing less, dance less, and play the keyboard, less. However, I express myself creatively through singing, writing, and dancing.

It's just not a side of myself that I shared with everyone. Although, as I grow older, I am becoming less inhibited. I guess you could say I get my creative side from my father. During one of my conversations with my dad (when he was healthy), he told me I would write a book and asked me what the title would be. I did not put serious thought into what he was saying at the time. But here I am, at least a decade later, contributing a chapter to a book about daddy-daughter issues.

My earliest memory of my father is when I visited my paternal grandfather's home. As I entered the front door and proceeded to walk through the living room to the kitchen, I could hear someone playing the piano. That someone called out, "Adrienne, Do you know who I am?" I replied, "No." and kept walking. I vaguely remember him calling me over and telling me he was my father. I do not remember how I felt or responded.

I can only imagine the pain he felt, having his daughter not know him. The lack of memory of my feelings at the moment signifies a numbness I felt throughout my early childhood and as an early teen. That numbness did not take voice until my later teenage and young adult years.

I remember having a tantrum as a young girl crying out in my bed, "I want my dad or daddy." I vaguely remember having some disagreements with my mother, which resulted in me retiring to my room. I chose to chant those words until I fell asleep. This would be the beginning of what I now know as my escape to a phantom father or night and shining armor who could/would come and save me when I needed comfort that I could not receive from my mother or someone else.

I remembered a few conversations on the phone with him at that young age. I remembered receiving a letter from him in which I received my first $20 bill. The following sum of money I would get from him would be when I was an adult due to his passing. That money would later be used as a down payment on the home I live in today. It was not until I was in my (a lady never tells her age) that I realized that my father did provide me with something. I thanked my Heavenly Father the moment He brought it to memory.

However, Robert Sanders (my father) was not a steady presence in my life. I can count (on one hand) the number of conversations we had and the number of times we were in each other's presence. His absence led me to question why he was not in my life as a little girl. At eight years old, I reasoned with myself that he was not in my life because he did not love me, nor did he find me important enough to be in my life.

That belief system transformed into "I am not important, I am not loveable by a man, I am not worthy, and I am not enough." That little girl's belief system ran my life well into adulthood. That belief system caused me to question my worth and value in every area of my life. That belief system affected all my relationships: familial, friendships, colleagues, romantic, etc.

I did not make this connection until I did my healing work as an adult. I did not realize my sadness or depression was linked to my father's absence until he was fatally ill and nearing his death bed. During the second to last conversation I had with my dad, I articulated this idea to him. In the last conversation with my dad, I prayed for him on his deathbed. He was scared and did not know me. He called out to his girlfriend for comfort, and not long after that, he passed.

As a little girl in grade school, I hid by not speaking or socializing. Finally, I was so quiet that one of my teachers encouraged my mom to take me out of the public school system and put me in a smaller private school setting, so I would not slip through the cracks.

My mom followed her advice. It was hard to go unnoticed in the small private school. I had a few outlets which allowed me to express myself: ballet dancing and musical dancing performances. These new opportunities were provided to me through the principal of the school, who was a former ballet dancer. The principal was one of my public school long-term substitute teachers who taught me how to make props and choreographed Broadway-like musical dance performances.

When I started junior high, I was just as quiet but did happen to make a few friends. In high school is where I was introduced to my Heavenly Father. I began to develop a personal relationship with Him. I remember one of my junior high school teachers bringing up the topic of fathers. She said that she felt sorry for anyone who had not grown up with their father and said something about the importance of that relationship.

I remember getting defensive and saying that I did not have my father, and I was doing just fine with my mom. My mother was doing an excellent job, but I believe that day brought an awareness of a void in my life. It could have been days, weeks, or months after that impromptu topic of conversation as I remember walking to school in tears, crying out to God about a void that I felt. Somehow, I could verbalize the emptiness I felt due to my father's lack in my life. As clear as day, I remember God telling me that He was my source and that only He could fill my void.

I would wrestle with this idea through high school, college, and the early years of my career. I began to yearn for the attention and love of a boy/man to feel what I now know is validated. However, I was scared to socialize with the male species. So I began to base my worth on them giving me attention or lack thereof.

I sunk deeper and deeper into my bubble to the point where I honestly thought I had become invisible. In order to have friends, it seemed that I would have to be the one to initiate. I wanted so badly for someone to initiate a friendship with me. Then finally, one day, a gentleman showed interest, but he showed interest in all the girls, is what I would say to myself. I also was honestly not attracted to him. However, he was the first boy to pursue me and saw me for me. I know that now, but I rejected it as a teenager.

Another gentleman chased me when I was a teenager, but he chased other girls on my block. He seemed to be an intelligent, respectable young man, but all he wanted was to be touchy-feely when I gave him attention. As a young woman of faith, I prided myself in being abstinent, so he stopped chasing me when I would not give in. This also brought awareness to the lack of fight or voice when a young man wanted me for physical reasons. But unfortunately, it also developed a type of shame. The touch felt good, but at the same time, I wanted to please God and stay away from any physical contact with a man.

A couple of gentlemen pursued me in college, but they were touchy-feely. They could not communicate. That did not make me feel valuable at all. I tended to like the young men who were spiritual leaders or a leader in some facet. However, they did not seem to like me in that way. We were good friends or acquaintances, but they continuously pursued other girls for their girlfriends. My friend group went on an outing one day. Everybody was coupled up except for one of my male friends (who I thought was a leader, very mature, and spiritual) and me. The girls walked ahead, and the guys were a few steps behind. I overheard his best friend say, "what about Adrienne" and he said, very quickly, I might add, "No, Nahhhhhh." That's all I can remember now. But, his indirect rejection played in my head throughout that day. I played it off for the rest of the day as if I was good, but I was not.

I later mustered up enough courage to confront my friend about why he responded in that way. He answered that I needed to show what I had to offer. (Well, that's all I can remember). What did I have to offer? What did that even mean? That played through my mind for quite some time. I did not know what I had to offer. Therefore, that left me feeling even more empty and unlovable.

His response started my victim mentality and solidified my belief that I was unworthy of a man's love. After that, I couldn't catch a break. I was not attracted to the guys that were attracted to me. They seemed to be after my body, and the Christian guys felt like I had nothing to offer.

At the end of my college journey, all my friends were engaged. When I came back home to start my adult life, my void was far more significant. I felt so alone. God's words to me as a teenager played through my spirit (I am your source. Only I can fill your void. You will ONLY be satisfied by me).

But at that moment, I decided I needed something tangible. Therefore, I started settling and gave a couple of young men, who I would typically not give the time of day, a chance. I broke my vow to be abstinent with my first boyfriend as a young adult and made all kinds of poor choices.

My departure from being a virgin was against my will. I did not want to do it. I cried, and I said No, but then I was silenced by the fear of being alone and not being enough for any other man. But after a while, I ended my relationship with him due to the messiness of the relationship. Finally, I could not take it anymore, and I felt guilty concerning my Heavenly Father and my choices.

I began my teaching career and met a young Christian man who seemed very interested in me. He was a gentleman. We talked pretty often, to the point where I felt I needed to confess to him about my previous relationship and not being a virgin. He then told me his pastor told him to leave me alone, and he disappeared out of my life. I feel like I was ghosted (before that was even a term) because I thought we were having a conversation and being honest and transparent with one another. I never got the impression that our budding relationship was over, but one day he just stopped answering my phone calls, and that was it. That made me feel so unworthy. I tortured myself for not being a good Christian and losing out on what I thought was a good Christian man. So, I began to carry around the guilt of not being good enough for a good man and not being good enough in God's eyes.

The next gentleman that expressed interest in me would later be my husband and the father of my children. I chose to marry him despite his religious differences and other core differences. I desperately wanted to be loved by a man. I spent 19 years fighting to be seen, known, and loved in my marriage. I spent 19 years in this relationship fighting to be seen, known, and loved. I spent 19 years in this relationship trying to right my wrongs with God. As a result, I spent 19 years almost losing myself completely. In fact, this relationship mirrored everything I felt about myself: unlovable, unworthy, and unimportant. I received no compliments, was not affirmed, and was only verbally told that I was loved 2x's throughout my entire relationship.

My partner was very aware of my father-wounds and would say many times in the early part of our relationship that he could not and would not fill the void of me being fatherless. Although I now understand that he truly would not have been able to fill the void, at the same, the constant badgering of him telling me what he could not and would not do just made me feel so abandoned, uncovered, unprotected, uncared for, and unloved.

Throughout my 19-year relationship, I was on my career journey as an educator. I navigated through feelings of not being enough as a friend, acquaintance, teacher, leader, and every other title I had. It was quite a torturous feeling of being inadequate at every turn.

I felt like I was in a loveless relationship. My fear of disappointing God by breaking up with my partner and fear of my daughters not having a relationship with him kept me bound to the point where I came to the realization that I could do bad all by myself and my heavenly father loves me and does not want me to be miserable. I also realized that trying to stay together for the girls was not working because they were witnessing our toxic relationship and receiving some of the unhealthy behavior.

I had to put myself and my girls first. So, I ended the relationship. Once I separated from my partner, and he moved out. I felt like that 15 or 16-year-old girl again. I felt alone and cried for my fatherless daughter-wounds to be healed. I did a little more meddling, trying to do things myself, but I came to the point where I fully surrendered to God. I cried out to God for help and slowly started positioning myself to trust God as my source.

My self-love journey involved enrolling in landmark classes, attaining my (own) personal life coach, doing a self-guided confidence program, and diving into the scriptures and prayer. Landmark helped me realize that I lived a life based on stories that I told myself concerning my different interactions and relationships with people. I realized the stories that I had been telling myself put me in the position of being a victim and everyone else in the role of being a villain.

During that three-day session, I made a list of people that I was estranged. Then, I talked to every one of them, confessing my part in the breakdown of our relationship and freeing myself of the bitterness that I had. I even wrote a letter to my dad, but I do not believe I made the connection that my lack of self-esteem was the root of not having my father in my life.

At the time, I thought it affected my relationship with men whom I was afraid to talk to (yes, even though I was married for nineteen years). I would later learn that my whole being and how I viewed myself/showed up in the world stemmed from the story I created as a little girl about why my father was not in my life. My life coach helped me get out of my head and create the life I wanted.

The biggest accomplishment that I could bring to fruition was getting my master's degree. I started with a dual focus on Adolescent Literacy and Trauma Resilience but solely focused on Trauma Resilience. I considered those courses to be very expensive therapy sessions because I learned so much about myself and people in general. However, those courses helped me understand the choices I have made in life. They helped me understand people in general, and they helped me develop compassion for my students as a middle school teacher and my daughters as a mother.

My purpose began to shift after taking the Landmark and Trauma Resilience courses. I wanted to help youth and women gain the breakthrough and mindset shift I had gained. In addition, my confidence coach enabled me to do some shadow work and talk to the little girl within. All of these support systems helped me to get stronger and helped me to embrace myself, and see myself as God created me.

I later enrolled in an activating your purpose class where all the inner healing work had come to a head. I remembered when I created the story about why my dad was not in my life and realized that I had allowed that little girl to run my life for over three decades. I then participated in a speaking boot camp and a coaching program to become a life coach. Through the life coaching program and a Christ-centered life coaching business program, I did intensive work to reflect on the process I went through to get to the other side of healing so I could design my own coaching program and support youth and women in their healing journey. My journey took almost two decades, mostly because I was trying to do it by myself for most of those years. But once I surrendered to God and cried out for help, he strategically placed people in my life to support me, allowing me to get to the other side of healing much more quickly. My purpose was birthed through my pain, and I am here to serve youth and women who are tired of being stuck in their trauma stories and ready to begin their healing journey.

I am no longer a victim, and I am Victorious by Design. God validates me! I have everything I need. I can do anything I set my mind to do. God is truly my protector, provider, and source of everything I need. However, I know that when I allow my focus to stay on my disappointments, I will go into default and seek a phantom father (man) to be my knight and shining armor. So, when I catch myself doing that, I have to change my mindset and focus on my blessings.

I must tap into my power to create and lean on my Heavenly Father, my true knight in shining armor. Don't get me wrong, I desire a companion and husband, but after many failures from trying to find him myself, I trust God to allow us to cross each other's paths allowing us to meet when it's the right time. So, in the meantime, I'm praying for both our healing journey and preparation.

I am now a happily divorced mother of two beautiful young adult women. We are all healing, positioning, and growing into the women God intended us to be. Our healing journey breaks generational curses as far back as my mother's generation.

I thank God for placing me in my mother's womb and for placing my daughters in my womb. Together, we are a powerful Godly force. We are here to make a GREAT impact on the world. God is using us to help set the captives free!

If you can relate to any part of my journey and you are ready to do the work of getting to the root of your trauma story, reframing your trauma story, acknowledging God as your source, and discovering who you are from a God-worthy lens so you can experience the victory, I would be honored to walk alongside you and help you get to the other side of healing.

Adrienne Conyers-Bey
You are Victorious by Design!
*Not A Survivor, But A Thriver
Be Victorious

ABOUT THE AUTHOR

ADRIENNE CONYERS-BEY
An educator for the Philadelphia School District
Founder of Victorious By Design with Coach
Adrienne; Life Coaching Practice

Adrienne is a woman of faith, and her Creator and Heavenly Father are her sources. She has been blessed with two daughters (Deja and Ayanna). Adrienne is a 7th and 8th-grade middle school teacher and a Trauma Life Coach. She worked for the School District of Philadelphia for 20+ years and has spent all but one year of her career in the same school. Due to personally witnessing a shift in the student's and families' mental and behavioral health in the classroom, things went from manageable and thriving to unmanageable and surviving. As a result, she obtained her Master of Education with a minor in Trauma Resilience to better understand and support her students and families.

Attaining her master's degree was a possibility created while working with her personal Life Coach. Her experience with her life coach ignited a passion for serving youth and women in the same way, which led to her participation and completion of life coach training through the Focus of Love Signature Life Coach Program.

Adrienne is available to do a 6–8-week Trauma Resilience course for middle school youth and women.

Adrienne is available to do one-on-one coaching with women who are ready to reframe their trauma stories by viewing life from a God-lens in order to experience victory.

Email: victoriousbydesign.cchadrienne@gmail.com

Direct: 267.997.8792

Social Media: FB @Victorious by Design w/Coach Adrienne

CHAPTER TWO

A Family Secret

BY DR. LIZ BLANDING

I was planning a funeral for a man (James) with whom I have no connection other than the fact that I was told he was my father. I further solidified that this man was not my father. I felt nothing but numbness and confusion while stepping up. Two weeks had passed since he died. Not one of his other children, mothered by various women, would take on the responsibility of making his final arrangements and settling his estate.

My younger sister and I were hands in hand and arm in arm when she agreed to accompany me to sort out his affairs. We learned who he was during this unwanted process and closed the final chapter of his life. As we approached his apartment in a retirement community, we were given the keys to enter. It was a small dark dust dwelling with a ton of stuff to sort out. As we began looking for insurance policies, bank statements, and clues on starting, we finally came across bank statements.

After opening the envelopes, my sister and I were shocked to see that the accounts were joined, and she was a joint owner. Next, we discovered a small life insurance policy. After further researching, we found that she was the policy's sole beneficiary. As we uncovered each piece of this man's puzzling life, the details became odder and odder. I could only wonder if these discoveries were answers to the dark secret our family was desperate to keep hidden.

The stories that we grew up with no longer made sense. I had questions about many stories of my life. I was so confused but dared not utter a word to raise questions about what did not make sense.

I was told that the man (Mr. B.) that raised me was my father, who nick-named me Smiling Faces. He said that he had never seen anyone cry and smile at the time. If you are wondering, yes, I was nick-named after the song recorded by The Temptations. That's when the Motown sound swept the airways out of my hometown of Detroit, Michigan.

More about Mr. B later in the story. Growing up in our family, the children, no matter how old, were to be seen and not heard. This was very difficult for me. I have always had an inquisitive nature, coupled with being a literal person, which begot me many punishments and whippings as a child. As a result, I grew up feeling very misunderstood. No one understood me, especially my parents.

Let's go back to the beginning. I was taught fear from inside my mother's womb. My mother's first husband was an abuser. He is James (from the first paragraph, the beginning of my story). He was a 35-year-old truck driver that married a scared 18-year-old girl running from an abusive mother. She often told us it was marrying him or going to the army. Once she (my mother) left her mother's house, there was no going back. She chose to marry James, a man she barely knew. He abused her from the moment she said, I do. My mother discovered that James lied about his age, and he was recently released from prison. This instilled a deep-rooted fear in my mother. In the '60s, a woman had no voice. My mother did what her husband told her to do without question. When she got out of line, he beat her. She often expressed that all she wanted was a baby of her own—someone she could love and receive love back in return.

After enduring many years of abuse, neglect, infidelity, and humiliation, my mother found comfort in another man's arms. After a few months into the affair, she became pregnant and walked away from the relationship, never telling her lover she was pregnant. During the pregnancy, her husband, James, continued to get drunk, beat her, kick her down flights of stairs, drag her and abuse her in every way he could.

The growing infant inside of my mother was me. Research states that documented abuse of a mother can negatively affect the growth and development of an unborn child. The changes in the mother's stress levels can cause damage to the brain of a child in the womb. High levels of the hormone cortisol are a neurotoxin.

Research states that emotional abuse can affect a child's emotional development, including feeling, expressing, controlling emotions, lacking confidence, or causing anger problems. As a result, the child may find it challenging to make and maintain healthy relationships later in life. I now understand how much truth there is in these statements.

I have lived and worked through these effects my entire life. I can only remember a few blurred instances of my childhood, most of which were my mother screaming for James to stop beating and punching her. I still remember the feeling of shaking profusely and peeking from behind the bedroom door, crying helplessly in terror while witnessing the abuse on different occasions.

Most of my early childhood memories have been buried lines of forgotten memories. Yet, I wish I could forget that horrifying day. I was age three when I was standing, trembling, and holding my baby sister's hand, watching James (my mother's estranged husband) stabbing her repeatedly until she lost consciousness and fell to the living room floor. My sister and my blood-soaked little fingers gripped one another as tightly as possible. My mother's warm blood splattered over our little faces. If it had not been for the fact that we were visiting a relative, I might not be here today to share this story of my dysfunctional beginning.

The sirens from the emergency responders, police, and fire trucks came screaming down the street, and the rest is a fogged memory. My mother survived the stabbing. My sister and I survived the stabbing physically. However, the psychological and emotional effects went unaddressed.

Doctors told our family that the knife missed my mother's temple by ½ inch. Any closer, the wounds would have been fatal.

After being released from the hospital, my mother, sister, and I went into hiding. James was never caught and was never officially charged by police for his vicious, deliberately cruel attack. I know, I know, you want to know more about what led up to the day of the stabbing. Well, you must understand that it has taken me over fifty years to unpack, unscramble, and be able to share this horrible memory with anyone. If you hang on in here with me, I promise I will get you caught up to this point. Now let's get back into the story.

The whispers at family gatherings, especially holidays, kept me feeling deceived, unprotected, and unsafe. You know that nagging feeling that won't go away. The one that tells you something just is not right. I knew a deep family secret existed, but I had no idea everyone knew the secret except me.

My mother's side of the family incited arguments within the family that would become loud and extremely violent, including the use of knives and guns. As a child, my place of safety was underneath the table. I would imagine becoming an adult and having a voice, a choice of how my life would be. I was going to protect my children no matter what. I was not going to let them live in fear. As the years passed and I witnessed the abuse of alcohol in our family, this gave me the notion that alcohol and substance use was some sort of rite of passage into adulthood. I learned to suppress my emotions, live in the fight, or flight mode, self-medicate and smile my way to the other side of bad situations.

Being an overweight baby was cute. Being an overweight toddler with chubby legs was even more adorable, so they said. However, being an overweight teenage girl made me the subject and butt end of many of my family's fat jokes.

There again was no protection. A father is supposed to protect his daughter. Yes, my stepfather was there for me in many ways. He was a provider, a house protector, and an advisor. However, he did not protect me from even his demeaning fat girl jokes. I had to forgive him and the other family members, including my grandmother, for hurting me and not protecting me. Ignorance kept them from understanding that every joke, cruel comment, criticism, and the negative remarks were tearing down my self-esteem, confidence, and self-worth.

A father is responsible for loving his daughter and ushering her into her adult life as a confident well-loved, protected, balanced, educated, knowledgeable young woman with the skills and ability to make good, sound decisions. A father's treatment of his daughter teaches her how a man should treat her. He is her first love. However, that was not my story. I hated walking in the door of our home for fear of being subjected to negativity and ugly name-calling by the adults that should have guarded me against the pain, shame, and belittling. Don't get me wrong; this was not an everyday occurrence. However, it happened enough that it damaged me. The names left deep wounds and scars that followed me into my adulthood. In other words, I developed a heavy load of emotional baggage that weighed heavy on my mind, body, soul, and spirit.

I, "Smiling Faces," continued my journey into adulthood, dragging along the family secret that I was not privileged to know. I was often called the space child by my mother. I was different and did not fit in. Nevertheless, I marched by the beat of my own drum. I wanted more and knew that life had more to offer. My baby sister, who was two years my junior, was diagnosed with Lupus along the journey. The worst form of which attacked her organs, mainly her kidneys. Around age thirty, I decided to test as a possible kidney transplant donor for my sister. After lengthy discussions, she and I agreed to talk to our mother.

My sister was bold with a dash of unfiltered humor. Her question to my mother went something like this "Hey ma, before we get tested for this kidney transplant, tell us the truth. Are either of us basters?" After a long pause, my mother looked at me and replied, YES!!! She then looked toward the floor in utter shame and embarrassment. Pandora's box, which held the family's secret, had been opened.

Our mom admitted that she did not know who my father was. Silence filled the room. My stomach sank, and my sister and I stood silent, looking deeply into one another's eyes. Growing up, we teased one another about having different fathers, not knowing the truth.

My sister was a darker shade of black girl magic than I. Finally, the dots were starting to connect. A flood gate of questions began to rush into my mind. The family secret was finally revealed. All the years of hiding the truth could no longer be hidden. What now? Where do I go from here? Until that moment, I did not know that not knowing who my biological father was really made a difference.

I grew up with a loving stepfather who was an imperfect human being who was pretty amazing. He stood in the gap and took on a single divorced mother with two small daughters. He raised us as his own. I was expected to be okay and content that the father who raised me was not my father. And the abusive man, my mother's x-husband, who hunted me in my sleep was not my father, then who was my father?

The confusion continued as my mother's shame kept her silent. I continued to ask her questions every chance I got when I was alone with her. I waited until she was in a light enough mood and willing to talk to me. I had to brace myself for conversations with my mother as they would quickly turn negative. We had a tumultuous relationship, never really understanding one another. I blame it on the family secret. Maybe if I had known the truth, my mindset would have been different.

I waited for a nice summer day; you know, the day when the warm sunbeams through the window with just enough breeze to relax you. Yes, that kind of a day. I began the conversation with my mother, slowly asking who my father was. She took a couple of deep breaths and started telling me the story of how bad her marriage to James was and why she was not sure who my father was. She went deeper into the details and became more graphic about the pain she endured.

My mother explained she had taken a job at a local laundry mat to get some time away from her husband, the house, and her life. She loved her job and the opportunity to learn new skills and meet new people. She started to feel like her own person, making her own money and not feeling like someone's property.

She met a sweet, kind, loving, handsome, well-spoken man there. As time went on, an affair ignited. After a few months, she became pregnant. In extreme fear, she quit her job and disappeared, retreated home, and was out of the reach of her mystery man. He searched for her; however, he was unsuccessful in his quest to rescue her having little information about her. She never spoke to him again, and he never knew she was pregnant.

After I was born, there was a noticeable problem. I was fair-skinned-complexion while my mother and her husband were dark-dark-skinned complexions. As the story goes, when they brought me home from the hospital, her husband snatched me from her arms. He ran me down to his aunt's house and asked her if it was possible for two dark-dark-skinned-complexion people to give birth to a fair-skinned-complexion baby with red ears.

In those days, family members rallied to weather the storms of marriage and stay together. No one knew what his aunt told him. However, he was pleased with her answer and immediately dropped the matter. Unfortunately, the abuse continued when he was in town. He was required to travel as an over-the-road truck driver from state to state.

Two and a half years later, pregnant with her second child, the abuse accelerated. After giving birth, my mother decided that it was time to leave the marriage. She needed a plan. She needed help. While her husband was on one of his many trips out of town, my mother and aunt went out to have some well-needed fun. She met Mr. B. He was tall, handsome, and fun. Their sexual promiscuity was supposed to be a one-night stand. That one night turned into one more night, one more night, and one more night. They became inseparable. He vowed to get her out. However, he had to be just as careful. He was in a failing marriage and wanted out as well. They devised a plan to get my mother safely out and away from her abusive marriage, and then he would follow shortly after.

The night of her escape, she was to grab as much as her arms could hold, load the car that Mr. B was in, and they would never return. Then, unexpectedly James pulls into the driveway. My mother locked the front door and ran to the backdoor. James was outside the house, running from door to door. He ignored the car in front of the house. Finally, my mother ran out the front door in a mad dash to the running vehicle where Mr. B, my sister, and I waited for her. James jumped in front of the car in a rage, beating the hood of the car, yelling profanities and threats. Mr. B hit the gas pedal and ran James over.

Here is where my mother, sister, and I went into hiding for the first time. Looking over our shoulders became a new way of life. The word on the street was that James was looking for us and would kill my mother when he saw her again. He told everyone in the neighborhood that he would see her dead and his children in foster care before letting her go.

Time had passed when James spotted my mother at a relative's house and asked to talk with her. But unfortunately, my mother made the mistake that many women make. She trusted a dangerous predator. I will never forget that day. That day, James attempted to keep his word and create a blood bath with my mother's blood for his two little girls to witness.

I believe this is the day that set the tone for my life, having fear and unsafe feelings. As we learned earlier, my mother, my sister, and I escaped the stabbing and were able to walk into a new life. My mother offered up bits and pieces throughout the years, never confirming or denying that her mystery lover was my father. As my mother continued to give me more details about my life, she would check the pulse of our numerous conversations. She did not want me to stop loving her or think ill of her because of what she had done. I assured my mother that my need to know more did not change my love for her. I told her that I believed every child has the right to know both sides of their family. I strongly expressed that I believed that every child has the right to know their father. Let me emphasize that by saying only in cases where the child would be safe meeting and knowing their father.

I asked my mother about fragmented memories of that day when I was fourteen. My uncle stopped by. He told my mother a man from her past had been shot and killed during a drug store robbery. It was her mystery man. I remember that day being sad and my mother crying endlessly. Then, finally, she said yes, it was him. I was so angry. For fourteen years of my life, the opportunity to know him was gone for no explainable logical reason. He had children, a daughter older than I and a younger son. A family secret kept too long to hide shame and guilt is crippling and does more harm than good. The innocent child is caught in the middle and hurt for no intelligent reason.

By saying okay, that's enough; my mother often stopped the conversations allowing me to collect no information. Unfortunately, the past is the past, and some things should go to the grave with us. My independent searches to find answers all turned up void. I did not have enough information. As I continued my journey, I did not qualify to be a kidney donor for my sister. She finally received two kidney transplants that lasted for a few years each and ultimately failed. My sister passed away two weeks before her 40th birthday.

As I look back over my life, I understand the devastating effects that family secrets can have on the life of a tiny innocent baby girl when she is left unprotected. The very thing that little girls look to their father for is protection. But, when the walls of safety are missing, a little girl grows into a fearful, naive woman. She starts searching for love while suffering over and over again at the hands of predators. The sad part is that she can't see herself clearly due to her fogged, underdeveloped perceptions of life and people. I call my failed marriages and abusive relationships lessons and blessings. But, the blessings in it all are that I have learned from each and never have to make the same mistakes and poor judgment calls ever again.

For me, the turning point was no more pain and getting rid of the emotional baggage blockers that weighed heavy on my soul. Instead, I used work and love as my drug to cover up the pains of my past. I used to work because I was damn good at it. I was in control. I used to love because it made me feel good. It made me feel safe until it did not.

Research has shown that falling in love is much like the sensation of feeling addicted to drugs. The euphoria, including brain chemicals like dopamine, **oxytocin**, adrenaline, and vasopressin, became addictive because the little girl that witnessed and suffered violence and abuse was never protected. I was never taken care of, and I never felt safe or protected. I was innocently, however, willingly used by predators because I was seeking acceptance while crying out for help with my mouth shut, crying with "Smiling Faces."

I hit a brick wall. It was actually a tree at the top of an expressway embankment. One icy, snowy morning in rush hour traffic, a car hydroplanes into my truck, flinging me, my mother, and my passenger three lanes over and up into a tree street level. When I regained consciousness, my head was smashed into the airbag. I looked over at my mother, and she was not moving. One leg was hanging out of the door. I jumped out of the car wearing high-heeled boots and walked behind my truck, which was on an incline, to reach the other side to help my mother. When I reached her, she asked me if I thought the truck was going to roll. I looked down at the gear shift, which was still in drive. I snatched my mother to the ground. The tree's grip on the truck loosens a split second later; the car rolled backward, down onto the expressway. The speeding oncoming traffic hit and totaled my car.

We stood at the top of the hill, my mother crying her eyes out, yelling and screaming, Lord, we can't take anymore. I jumped up and down, vomited air and stomach fluid, and thanked God for saving us. We were in traffic that morning going to probate court to gain guardianship over my stepfather, who had been slipping into the darkness of dementia for the past ten years. We had recently buried upward of eight close family members. Now we are the backbone of the family, sitting on the side of a snow and ice-covered hilltop. It was a cold winter morning, and we were unaware of the pain that followed the bang-up that we survived.

We watched the emergency responders, police officers, and tow truck drivers clear the accident. Then, the police officers had to figure out how to get us down from the top of the hill to get medical attention. There was a fence separating the grass and trees from the pedestrian side of the street.

After waking up a few days later, when the adrenaline rush had worn off, my body was in excruciating pain. As time when on, I endured every type of therapy, including occupational therapy, physical therapy, psychotherapy, and manipulation under anesthesia, to regain mobility in my body and limbs.

Doctor after doctor, specialist after specialist, told me I had plateaued and would not get any better. Finally, I knew it was time for me to work on myself. I refused to believe that it was all over for me. I was a single, divorced mom with too much to accomplish. My children needed me to get better. I remember repeating aloud to my doctors, myself, and anyone willing to listen. My current situation is not my destiny.

God showed me more about my purpose and life than the prognosis the doctors wanted me to accept. I refused to believe I would be wheelchair-bound if I did not have double knee replacement surgery. I refused to think that I would never be able to regain a thriving lifestyle ever again. No, I was not hearing it nor was I going out like that. I went to work. Traditional medical professionals told me that I would not get any better if I did not accept where I was. I remember telling myself that I would not get any better if I accepted what the doctors told me.

As I was sitting at home watching the replay of my truck rolling back down into traffic and after being saved from a horrific car accident like that one, it was time to get a grip and stop repeating the same mistakes over and over again in my life's journey. It was time to realize that no one was coming to save me! No one was coming to make me feel safe! No one will save me but me and my faith in God! I had to protect the little girl inside of myself. I had to thrive and not just survive. So, I surrendered my victim mentality, gave up my survivor title, and exchanged them for a badge of honor as a Thriver.

When pivoting from pain to gain, there must be a shift. I am a literal, visual person. For me, a transformation or change may look a little drastic to someone else; however, this is my story to write and tell. I was born Mary Elizabeth Coston. However beautiful for some, that name represents a lifetime of tremendous pain for me. For me to shift from pain to power, it took something drastic. It took something that would remind me daily to stand up for that little girl that was never protected. It took me to draw a line, like a circle with the bright red line standing for no more of this or that. The name change from Mary to Liz was what it took for me to pivot.

I suffered from feelings of low self-esteem and low self-worth while making poor decisions. I was seeking validation from men while ignoring the obvious red flags. I indulged in risky behavior, and I did not see the beauty in myself that everyone else saw in me. As a result, I suffered from loneliness and fear of rejection.

The healing process had begun, and I needed to hit the refresh button on life. I desperately needed to walk out of my painful, traumatic past. A rebirth, a new me, needed to emerge. I knew I was created to be, do, and have my heart's desire. No more victim experience! My future was a new life, full of possibilities, high frequency, and illuminating guiding light. Mary, Mary sang about No More Tears, and I declared no more tears.

I began my studies in the Naturopathic world of herbs. I became my first client. And baby, did I have my hands full. It's okay to chuckle; I know I can be a bit much sometimes. So lean in; I chuckled too. I wanted to overcome the medical health challenges and learn to live with and better manage my deficiencies. I desperately wanted to relieve myself of the pain without using harmful drugs with side effects that scared me more than my condition. So, I immersed myself in the wonderful world of herbs. I studied and discovered a true passion for natural medicine.

A Special Note to My Heartbroken Daddy-Less Daughters

The daddy-less daughter issues in our family began when my great-grandfather was lynched. My great-grandmother (his wife) and children were forced off his land. This created a generation of daddy-less daughters. Why? I'm glad you asked. When a father's influence and love are absent from a daughter's life, her "Picker," meaning her ability to select a proper mate, is skewed by the need & desire to anesthetize her present pain. Generation after generation of women in our family has used love as a drug to feel good. We learned by exposure that we had no other choice. So, daughters' I am here to let you know you have choices. A choice to be with a man that will love you, care for you, protect you, cover you and grow with you.

Throughout my story's many adversities, I knew I was destined to find my seeds of greatness. May you find your seeds of greatness within my story. Remember, you are not alone. If I can thrive, not just survive, so can you.

- Dr. Liz Blanding N. D. "The Menopause Mama & The Asset Diversification Coach."

ABOUT THE AUTHOR

DR. LIZ BLANDING, N.D., NATUROPATHIC
WELLNESS COACH

Dr. Liz Blanding is a business owner driven by her passion for empowering and educating others in the arena of Natural Wellness. She is the Founder and C.E.O. of Oasis Wellness Centers, an online herbal wellness academy, and is affectionally named "The Menopause Mama." She helps menopausal women overcome the challenges of menopause with education and herbs.

She is also the Founder of Soothing Salve, an organic herbal blend of over 29 herbs designed to relieve aches and joint pain from sore, tight muscles and inflammation. In addition, she became business partners with the phenomenal Coach Michael Bart Mathews. Together, they created F.Y.M.O.C - the Finding Your Moment of Clarity transformational system. F.Y.M.O.C teaches entrepreneurs how to build, grow and scale their businesses. In addition, she is the published author of "ITS SMOOTHIE TIME," a fun book to kick-start your journey into making healthier nutritional choices that are mouth-watering and full of flavor.

Dr. Liz is a sought-after speaker, teacher, talk show host, and content creator of her Podcast "Oasis Wellness of Life, on YouTube, soon to be found on other major podcasting and radio platforms. Her most prized titles are that of a Mom of three beautiful adult children, two additional sons by marriage, and eight amazing grandchildren. Yes, she is a Grandma, aka Buca, aka Nana.

Dr. Liz has mentored, coached, and encouraged those in her circle to be the absolute best for many years. She learned the key to change was to mend her brokenness. So when she was invited to be a part of this amazing collaboration, Dr. Liz did not think twice. She was all in. For many years, deep down in her heart, Dr. Liz always knew her story was not meant for her suffering. The pain she suffered was not in vain! Her pain was not just for her to learn valuable lessons. She needed to learn to develop and transform into today's intentional, purposeful woman. Her pain was & is for the thousands of daughters that suffer in loneliness and silence.

Fathers play such an integral role in the life and development of daughters. Fathers are necessary. I applaud the fathers that love and create a healthy, safe environment for their daughters to grow, develop and flourish. I especially want to extend a special heartfelt thank you to the supportive, loving, caring men who champion women. Kings of Kings, I honor, respect, and salute you.

Dr. Liz Blanding, N.D. Schedule your appointment: www.https://linktr.ee/drlizblanding

The Menopause Mama and Asset Diversification Coach – 1.248.750.7231

Website: https://oasiswellnesscenters.vipmembervault.com/

CHAPTER THREE

Where Is My Daddy

ROBYN SMITH-HAYNES

The earliest memory I can think of with my father was about age three. He gave the best hugs! I remember we were in a car driving down a dirt road in the country. We were going to visit his mother, my grandmother, in Gonzales, Louisiana. The drive seemed to take forever because I remember I had to use the bathroom. I remember this memory vividly because I can still hear Stevie Wonder singing "My Cheri Amore" on the radio. It wasn't a fun ride because it was hot and sticky. I remember looking out the window, wondering where in the heck I was. I lived in New Orleans, Louisiana, with Betty and Sydnee. The setting was the mid-seventies, and things were very different back then. There weren't the safety concerns back then as we have in this time of the new millennium.

This single memory would cloud my head for the next six years. I thought this memory was a dream. My daily life with Betty and Sydnee mostly included thoughts of a daddy. My dreams were vivid and often included people I wished would be around, like a daddy.

Growing up in a family where no one discussed my daddy was brutal. But regardless, I wanted a daddy around me like everyone else. At age four, I remember my sister getting dressed. She was getting picked up by her daddy. Hearing this, I got excited and dressed up to meet our daddy. I had concluded that she was my sister, we had the same mother, so I figured I would be meeting our daddy.

Boy, was I way off the mark! I went to our living room dressed in a dress. Wearing a dress was significant because I was a natural tomboy.

I figured I had better get all gussied up to meet this daddy I'd never known. I sat on the sofa next to Sydnee, and we waited together. She was nine years older than me. We sat for a while, then Sydnee looked at me and wondered why I was dressed up. I told her I was waiting to meet our daddy! I was so excited, wearing my pretty dress, bow in my hair, wearing patent leather shoes that I had put on all by myself! I was so proud at that moment!

In one fell swoop, Sydnee yelled at me, saying, "we were not going with HER DADDY" and that she was going to spend time with her daddy. I was embarrassed and ashamed because I adored Sydnee and she pretty much became revolted at the thought of how I was imposing on her life with her daddy. I got off the sofa and hid in the closet, crying until Sydnee left with her daddy.

Betty came and found me and asked me why I was crying. She was not the most affectionate or compassionate person in the world. I told her what had happened before Sydnee left with her dad. I was sad because I didn't have a daddy. Without hesitation, Betty told me my daddy was dead and not to worry about a daddy because I had her and my uncles.

Man, What could I say? At four years old, when someone tells you a person is deceased, you believe them, right? So, I accepted the fact that I was fatherless. What else could I do? It came from Betty, who was Alpha and Omega, next to God! As the years progressed, we lived in a rigid home, and we had a rigorous weekly schedule. We attended a private catholic school and participated in school activities. Betty worked at NASA on the external fuel tank project, and it was church, church, and more! We are Baptist but attended Catholic school. By the way, my upbringing included more guilt and Jesus than the law should allow! We attended choir rehearsals in the evenings and on Saturdays because our church produced some of the best singers in the city! We would perform at the New Orleans Jazz and Heritage festival mostly every year and sing in the gospel tent. We met some greatest names in gospel music.

I was proud of my family even though there was a void in my world without a father. My life consisted of family visits with my grandparents, aunts, uncles, cousins, and other social gatherings. No one ever mentioned my father during those visits.

I had awesome uncles and aunts who loved me as if I were their child at times, which seemed normal. I loved my family, and they loved me. So, it was not strange not having a dad in my world. But, in my world, I felt complete, plus you can't miss something or someone you never had or knew before. So, I decided to roll with it and enjoy life without a daddy. It wasn't until I was about seven years old that I overheard a conversation with my grandmother and aunt about father's day.

I thought I was doing something bad by hearing them discuss me, not having a father in my life, and how I would feel if my cousins were doing something special for their fathers or our grandfather. Kids have the attention spans of gnats. What I overheard was spotty at best. But I do remember how adamant my aunt was. It didn't make sense to me because my dad was dead, right? I never got closure from what I overheard, but it always stuck out like a sore thumb. Deep down, I guess I was trying to figure it out.

Anyway, I laughed it off. During this period in my life, I suffered some trauma that took me years to come to grips with. Families must pay attention to what is going on when kids are around. No one thinks or believes that kids can hurt or harm each other when no one is watching closely enough. That's how my childhood trauma began.

As larger families can have many kids, there are times when all the kids are gathered together, like during the summers when parents have to work. The aunts and uncles took turns getting all eleven grandkids from my family to take trips to the country or the beach for a family vacation. When we passed places like orphanages, my aunts and uncles would threaten us and send us there for being "bad." That was enough for me to "act right," at least for a little while. Considering all the kids, maybe four or five adults watched everyone. It was a lot of responsibility for my aunts and uncles.

This was the norm because our family was so close. I mean, close. Living within a three-block radius was close. I was one of the younger kids in the group. Things would be done to me that made no sense to a little kid, like being in what looked like compromising positions, fighting, or being mischievous.

I remember we were all in a room horse-playing around, and someone touched my butt. I never considered it wrong but wasn't sure what had just happened, so I ignored it. I was a little kid, and it didn't seem like some weird, isolated thing to me. Later that evening, I remembered seeing the person that touched me near my bed where I slept. I was confused as to what they were doing. Then, they touched me to see if I was asleep or not, and I freaked out. I froze. I couldn't scream, move or do anything. I had no words for what was happening to me. I stayed as stiff as a board until he left. Then, I got up and went to the bathroom because it hurt.

I was confused and scared. Scarred that if I told on him, I would get in trouble and be sent to the place for "bad" kids because I feared Betty and grandmother more than anything, and I didn't want to be sent to the orphanage. That's what I was thinking at the moment. I had no dad to take care of me but only my mom. So, I suppressed it.

It seemed like the moment I did not tell anyone; it started happening more and more. Whenever this person came over to our house or our grandmother's house, he bothered me. His actions expanded from touching, to penetration, to whatever he required me to do. In my mind, I thought this was some form of love or affection, and I was special. They abused me for years, and I kept quiet about it.

In some strange way, I didn't know what he was doing was wrong until it abruptly stopped. There was no warning, no nothing, and we didn't spend as much time with them anymore. At this point, I'm about eight or nine years old, and lives are changing. Betty met a man who said I would end up with a stepdad. I didn't care much about that, but I was excited about getting a stepdad. I felt like if my mom was happy, so should I be. However, I did not fully understand what was ahead of me.

Sydnee and my female cousin decided to introduce me to "my daddy" in the latter part of my ninth year of life. We attended a small private catholic school, and there was a roofing company resurfacing the roof. The men on our campus were identified by the hard hats and safety items worn daily.

One day, Sydnee and another woman brought me to the corner of the school and waved at this man on the roof. He waved back. Sydnee told me to wave at "my daddy." I'm looking at them like they were nuts because Betty told me "my dad" was dead. I think Sydnee and the other woman were scamming this man for some crazy reason. Why else would he be communicating with a stranger? The wave ended, and I headed back to class. I didn't think anything of the wave, but the man waited for me after school.

Sydnee and another woman stood with this man while I walked toward them. I was scared and confused. I looked at everyone like they were nuts because Betty said: "my dad" was dead! Not being rude and being from the deep south, I introduced myself to this man. He was friendly, smiled, and shook my hand. He asked if I liked school and if Betty was all right. Of course, I responded yes and yes. This would never have happened by today's standards, but 40 years ago, it actually did.

This man gave us some money and well wishes. He mentioned that he would be there for a few weeks until the roof was completed. I thought nothing of it and proceeded to get a snowball after school with this newfound money. I didn't mention this to Betty because Sydnee explained how it would make her angry. We tried to keep the peace at home. My mom would go all "Mommy Dearest" on us when she was enraged if our chores were not completed or homework was not done. We kept this meeting "my dad" to ourselves. I began to see this man who professed to be "my dad" every day before and after school for the next three months. I can't lie; it was good to have someone care about me differently. But it seemed as quickly as he swooped in, he swooped out. I didn't know how to process this empty feeling of loss or abandonment. Just when I began to feel happy and like everyone else, with a dad. Poof, He was gone.

Then hell began!!!

I was always used to disappointment because Betty worked all the time. Most of the time, Sydnee went with her dad, and I was with my grandmother or aunt. It was always home, church, or the grocery store at my grandmother's. It was all kinds of adventures with my aunt because she had no kids. With her, it was like having a good time. I went roller skating, to movies, fancy restaurants, or whatever; it ran the gamete. I never had the security of my caretaker other than my mom. So, I took whatever attention I could get from whomever I could get it. This was just how it was back in the seventies and early eighties. I had no choice but to accept it, or so I thought.

Then, one day the man I called a monster entered my life. A piece of shit that pretended to be one thing to her and a pervert to me. BASED ON WHAT I KNOW NOW, I figured out that some adults are desperate to find love and happiness from a man for fear of being and living all alone. I did not like this man, and I got terrible vibes from this monstrous person that entered my life. Yes, he made my skin crawl, and I couldn't understand what others saw in this dude.

I believed no one in the family liked him. It seemed to me that in nearly no time, he was a fixture in my life. I didn't like this new life. This dude was abrasive, rude, and pushy. This was not the usual type of environment I lived in. It started to show in ways that made everyone question his motives.

As time progressed, it was no strange occurrence for him to pick me up from school; ugh. After a long day at school, a long drive can put a kid to sleep. That's when it happened, he touched me in my private area, and I froze! I was trapped in the car. I was scared, alone, and not sure what would happen.

This monster smoked, drank, gambled, and pretended to be nice to others while he was abusing me. He told me not to tell anyone because they wouldn't believe me since I had told fibs. He said there was nothing I could do about it either. Shock and disbelief surged through me. He said he would hurt my family if I did tell, and I couldn't have that. He said since I had no daddy, no one would care. He was a cold and callous bastard.

Much worse abuse continued for the next three years. I pretended to be all right, but it began to tear me apart internally for years! I put on a brave face most times and tried to deal with the situation of continued mental, physical, and sexual abuse.

One day, I finally got fed up with this piece of shit for always taking advantage of me. I was tired of being constantly in a state of hate or disgust and doing what it took to stay away from this man. I feared everything that came at me until one day, at school, I was in 5th grade, they showed us a film called "Kids do tell."

I was amazed that someone had written and disclosed the trauma that was occurring in my life! I was not alone! Oh my God! I couldn't believe it. I didn't know what to do. There was a chance for this trauma to stop. I had to muster up the nerve to speak to someone. Who could that be? I decided to tell my teacher, who showed us the movie. This was the beginning of the shit show!

My teacher called Betty and asked her to come to school to discuss a few things. My mom, thinking I was failing her class, immediately called me into her room to find out what was happening. She was not the parent to have schools call her about her kids without an explanation! She demanded an explanation.

With a belt in mom's hand, I attempted to tell her what had happened to me. Betty was shocked. She always expressed that she was my mom and my dad! She said she was not going to let any lies befall her. She called her closest friend to discuss harming the perpetrator who lived in our home. The friend calmed her down and devised a plan to get the necessary information and decide based on that information.

The next day, we went to school to meet with my teacher to discuss the issues I had shared was rough at best!

I was raised in a strict, forceful, hurtful, and aggressive environment.

There were many days that I dreamed of having "my dad" around. Betty had a support network and friends, but our lives did not look like the families we knew or watched on television. Going to school the next day put a fear in me that I could never shake. Betty, the teacher, and another woman went into my school's fancy teacher conference room for the longest time. When they concluded, I didn't return to class and had a long day.

I went to the doctor to have all these tests and a vaginal exam. They discovered I didn't have a hymen, and Betty told the doctor that it could have been from falling off a horse at nine years old because I was in a brace for three weeks due to a hairline pelvic fracture. Next, I went to this office to talk to social workers and psychologists. They asked what seemed to be hundreds of questions. Finally, they gave me baby dolls and asked me to show them what had happened to me with the dolls. I obliged them. I wanted this psychological interrogation to be over.

I was poked and prodded and repeatedly asked the most humiliating questions differently. Then, finally, we got to go home. I was relieved and did not realize what was happening next.

If I had a daddy at this moment, I could only begin to imagine the levels of protection needed to be safe and secure. But I didn't, and I had to continue living in this hell. After that, however, my world shattered.

Shortly after the initial interrogation, many more were to follow. I now had a social worker. I had to discuss my ordeal with her repeatedly. Next, it seemed as if nothing had happened. Then one day, I was required to go to court, and I was dressed in my Sunday best. That was the day that shifted my life for the next two years. The perpetrator was arrested. I was removed from my home and sent to foster care. I was away from my family and anything I may have known.

It felt like I was being punished for telling the truth! This was crazy! This was not the outcome of the movie! I was supposed to go back home, and the perpetrator was supposed to leave! Instead, I was removed from my home and sent to live in a strange-looking place. This house was a place of hell in a ghetto in America. But this was a place that would house me for about two months, which seemed like an eternity. Before this, I lived in a house with my family. We had food and everything you could expect from a middle-class family.

The warden, I mean foster mother, was evil in my eyes. The social worker left me there with three other kids. They were like hyenas coming after me. I did not look like them, act like them, or relate to them. It was dangerous. I didn't go to school because they had to get me registered. So, I stayed at that foster house, with all its horrors, and I cried every day.

I was required to clean while being violently and verbally instructed. I prayed to get out of this insane situation. Death would have been better than this place because it seemed that no one would rescue me. Until one day, I thought I was dreaming. I was finished cleaning and looked up to see my uncle! A familiar face walked up to me, and I was so excited that I jumped into his arms. I was never letting him go!

The social worker walked up behind Quincy and addressed the devil herself to declare that I would be leaving their home immediately! Her words were freedom to my ears. Of course, I wasn't going home, but away from this hell was good enough for me! So, I did not let go of my uncle until we got into the car, taking me away from that evil place.

We made the long drive to my uncle's house, where my family greeted me, my grandmother, other uncles, aunts, and cousins but not Betty. That moment was disheartening, but relief from that designated hell was worth it. Quincy expressed to me why Betty was not there and her decision to stand by the perpetrator because she said that I was known for telling lies and at that time, she was convinced that this was a ruse that I was telling another lie.

So, I could only grasp what I understood and accept what I needed at that time. Quincy became my hero, and I was happy to do whatever was necessary to be safe and in a familiar environment. A week later, Betty, the social worker, and Sydnee came to Quincy's house to visit. We had an hour. It was like Christmas in my head because I was finally excited to see Betty and Sydnee. Regardless of the situational parameters. We were a few months away before Betty could have me at home for weekend visits. It was amazing that things started returning to normal, or so I thought.

Although this was a nefarious plot, Betty ended this process and returned our family to our home. She began to tell me that I could fix this whole situation if I told the social worker that I had lied. I resisted for as long as I could deal with it. At this point, I was worn down. All I wanted was for things to go back to normal. It wasn't until we were required to go to court, and I was on the stand, that Betty shared that she had dealt with me lying and coming up with fantastic stories at times. However, the lawyer asked her questions about my descriptions of intimate areas on her husband and how I would describe them with such detail. Betty said I probably snuck around the house when they were intimate and saw something. She also said that the perpetrator would sometimes walk around the house in his undergarments and fall asleep on the couch while watching movies in the living room.

The judge was not happy with her responses. However, a decision had to be made about my safety and well-being in the home. Betty was granted temporary overnight weekend visitations. This continued for months until she finally discussed how to "fix" this with me. I had to tell them I lied. So, back to court we went, and just like that, I told the judge I lied. We left the court in like 20 minutes. We drove home for what seemed to be victory. We ate dinner and changed clothes and then got dressed to go somewhere. I breathed a sigh of relief.

Imagine my disbelief when I was driven to pick up the perpetrator once again. I was devastated! I could not believe this was happening. As a child, we don't think very far ahead. As he entered the vehicle, He was happy, and I was not. My greatest fear was coming to fruition, facing this rotten bastard and the unknown plot he would release on me once we got home. I had never felt more defeated until this point.

Life changed, and he didn't touch me again. I took my stance and was ready if he would ever try to hurt me. I would have shut it down like John Wick or Kill Bill. Instead, I gained my power back from preparing mentally and physically to protect myself.

Years after this, I was responsible for a school project that required my birth certificate. I asked Betty for my birth certificate and found a folder with multiple copies. I felt strange when I noticed numerous documents with the current last name that I had gone through school with and then a different last name! Huh?

The confusion was real! I discovered my original birth certificate with my first name and another middle and last name that was not my current middle and last name. But the last name matched the father's last name. And on the copies with my current last name, there was no father's name. I asked Betty what the deal was regarding my birth certificate, and she gave me a copy with my current last name with no explanation. I was more concerned about upsetting Betty because discussions about my father were not warm and fuzzy conversations. I finally realized my daddy was a sore spot for Betty. At this point, the research began.

I went to my grandmother, and she explained how Betty and my father's relationship did not work out. My daddy would decide to leave instead of causing a scene or physical altercation with Betty. She laid it all out for me, and I was shocked! My daddy was a commercial roofer, and he traveled a great deal and had other children before me. That was a fact that Betty was not too happy about. My grandmother had two pictures of my daddy. To my surprise, the picture was the same man from the roof of my elementary school that my sister and my female cousin introduced me to when I was about nine years old!

At this point, I'm sixteen, in high school, and making my plans to leave Betty's house for college. I was an honor student, cheerleader, track star, and all-around good student. I took a job at the Audubon Zoological Garden gift shop. I was a superstar cashier who could make $1000 selling trinkets to kids and tourists on any given day. The zoo gift shops were the coolest places on the property. I was the envy of other workers because they worked in the heat! My world came full circle when this man entered my gift shop with a little girl who looked like a younger version of me on one hot summer day!

I could not stop looking in amazement at this little girl when the man called my name and said, I'm your daddy, and this is your baby sister. The shock was too much to handle. I turned around and called my grandmother to ask what was going on. She assured me that it was my father and my baby sister. She told him that I was at work and where to find me.

This was when the floodgates opened in my life. I shook my daddy's hand, and he pulled me in and gave me the biggest hug and told me how proud he was of me. I told him I had to finish my workday and leave work. When I got off work, I walked to the parking lot to find my daddy and my baby sister waiting on me. We got in the car, and he drove me home to my grandmother. I was initially scared, but in a good way. My dad spoke to me and told me all about my brothers and sisters. I was shocked. I was always the baby, and now to find out I was the middle child was wild!

Once we arrived at my grandmother's house, we sat down to talk. My grandmother explained that she knew where my father was but could not tell me because of my mom. My grandmother told me that she used to ask me for extra school pictures to give to my dad. I just thought she would lose or misplace them and never thought anything of it. Finally, my dad pulled out a scrapbook about three inches thick. He opened it and showed me every picture, the news articles, reports about my school, every honor roll, and public announcement about me at my schools and with my church. I was impressed and amazed that he kept up with me through my grandmother. I knew it was true because all the pictures had my notes that I would write for my grandmother. And I loved on them!

My daddy was so proud of me, and it showed. I was very nervous because this was like a dream was coming true. He told me my full name and why he wanted to be a part of my life. He felt that I needed to know the truth. I asked him why it took so long to come for me. He explained that it was very messy and complicated, that he knew I was in good hands as far as being raised and loved by Betty, or so he thought. But no one told him of the abuse and hurt I suffered.

He brought me to his home, where I met my stepmother and siblings. I found my tribe! I never fully felt like I belonged on Betty's side of the family. They didn't see things as funny or humorous as I did from thinking outside the box. They were not even seeing my entrepreneurial spirit as my father did. But, in life, things tend to happen to make us whole.

Those things tear us down or build us up, giving us perspective. I believe (for me) that day did all three. I found a new perspective once meeting, learning, and knowing my daddy. It tore down the lies I was living. I stopped questioning who I was and created healing in my life to help me discover who I actually could be.

Meeting my siblings redirected my perspective on what and who my family actually was. I found out my siblings knew all about me, and I knew nothing about them. This was crazy because it showed me that someone who loves you would share with who they love. I missed out on at least thirteen years of who I was. I missed out on knowing a man, my dad, who was one of the coolest cats in town. I legally changed my name and went to college with my real name. It was freeing to be released from the level of lies and tyranny that Betty swirled around me. I believe she was angry and hurt by my father leaving her when I was about two years old. Because of that void, I spent the next sixteen years learning more and yearning to learn this new side of my life.

I told my dad about the horrible things that happened to me. He told me he was sorry for not being there and showed this in his actions toward me. My daddy told me that he definitely would have killed that person if he would have had any idea what was happening to me. I told my dad I needed him to be here because I had too many years to learn how to be his daughter.

It was so much fun and a delight to know that I was no longer the girl without a daddy! He made it a point to participate. He made it to all my graduations, wedding, birthdays, and childbirths from then on. My dad became my hero, removing the void I used to feel has been placed on my mental backburner of memories.

No one would understand that their actions thwarted the opportunities that could have happened in a more positive way for me, I forgave them for their actions and realized they had their reasons for doing what they did.

Looking back, I finally was getting to live and learn who my father was, and the lessons he imparted in me transformed me into a better person. I'm a woman with daddy issues who has worked hard to dispel them and teach my daughters how learning better opportunities can help them grow and expand as a person.

My father showed me not to disconnect from family and what family truly is. The strength that my father gave me is evident in keeping me in a good space. Meeting my father gave me purpose at a time that I could not see. Meeting and engaging with my father's other children made me understand what I had missed. I missed him not being around. Their joyful memories allowed me to understand, much deeper, how my life could have turned out with my dad there.

Unfortunately, my dad contracted cancer and died in 2011 when I was 37 years old. My dad got the opportunity to watch me walk into womanhood, proud and secure in who I was. He saw me date men and gave me pointers. He advised me to make adjustments as needed to succeed in life. He watched me marry and birth his legacy to grow and impart life lessons as he did with me. It's been over ten years since losing my daddy. But, I can attest to having learned to say daddy with ease; I still have a constant and deep connection and communication with my siblings and believe I am a much better person for it.

At this point in my life, I see where my daddy's presence (when I was a youth) would have changed the trajectory of my life in a much great way. Yet, without the obstacles I experienced, I would not have had the opportunity to heal, grow and become the person I am and still growing to be. My daddy told me many things to help me be whole and work at being who I am as a person—making it worth the void to meet the fulfillment of what he birthed into this world. It has taught me to take advantage of opportunities because life is short. We owe ourselves to make the most of our time together because we cannot recoup time once it is gone.

My dad told me he was happy that I was open to meeting him and my baby sister that day. He was not sure if I would be alright, given all the information we had to work through to get to the best place in our relationship. My dad expressed how he longed to father me and give me a life worthy of God and the life we were supposed to live.

I only had my daddy for about 21 years from the day we finally met. I made up my mind to make every opportunity count as we grew to love one another and be happy with the connection that we had finally completed. My daddy was a remarkable man, funny, smart, flaws, and all. He never tried to be someone he was not and made sure I understood that principle in life.

Making solid family connections is a powerful thing. I've forgiven and released any grudges that were once deep in my psyche. I made room and did the work to get through the levels of hurt, guilt, and pain that could thwart continuing to be a better person. I realized I could have disconnected and remained on an island. But the chaos would have driven me completely mad. I think that daddies, the good ones, have an indescribable place here on earth.

Living in the daddy void without knowing who your daddy is, is not a positive way to exist. The impact it causes is deep-rooted, internally, externally, and emotionally, yet identifying the daddy void and working to grow through it has shown me that you can get better regardless of the pain and hurt one can experience in life.

I will forever cherish the experiences I received from spending quality time with my dad. He became a focal point in my world, which propelled me to a broader means of being whole. My daddy is also why I took a chance and developed my entrepreneurial spirit to create my own tax preparation business called All Aspects Tax Services, LLC.

Studying my dad's insight, heeding his principles and advice, and cultivating relationships with my siblings gave me the purpose to develop my grant writing and interviewing capabilities, which I utilize in my businesses. All things came together to build and brand a legacy that can sustain and last for many years to come.

Robyn Smith-Haynes

My dad, Robert "Junie Boy" Smith, Jr.

ABOUT THE AUTHOR

ROBYN SMITH-HAYNES

Robyn Smith Haynes is a single mother of 2 beautiful girls and has worked hard to give them a better life than she once knew. As a Network Systems Administrator in Atlanta, GA, by trade, she owns and operates multiple thriving companies. By utilizing the skills developed for tax preparation and tax planning, she birthed All Aspects Tax Services, LLC, and All Aspects Consulting, which is the grant writing and business consulting services arm of her companies.

Originally from New Orleans, she is a graduate of McDonogh #35 Senior High, attended Loyola University, graduated from Ashwood University in Humble, TX, and is currently working toward her Master's degree from Colorado Technical University. Living through the pandemic has afforded her voice to be heard by documenting and expressing her journey through poetry and short stories. She has found her way and experienced a fantastic voyage thus far and is looking to go to higher heights and farther depths in growing and developing more for the future.

All Aspects Tax Services was birthed out of drive and motivation to succeed in helping people maneuver their tax responsibilities. Robyn has been a certified tax preparer for more than ten years. By striving to provide all clients with the most valuable and accurate tax information to reduce their tax debt and possibly get them a refund. We offer tax planning services to get your business needs on the right track to be ready for each tax season.

We specialize in individual and commercial tax preparation. Please feel free to call us at 678-827-1075 to discuss your tax needs or email us at rhaynes.aats@gmail.com. #MoneyMagnet

Robyn Smith Haynes
All Aspects Tax Services

CHAPTER FOUR

The Decisions He Made

BY SAKINNA J

I was born June 1st, 1985, in Philadelphia, Pa. I was the second born then; my little sister came two years later, making me the middle child. My mother and father both worked as I was growing up. My mother mostly worked two jobs as she cared for me and my sisters full time, while my dad worked full time at a steel plant. My father lived with my stepmother in Norristown, Pa., while my sisters and I lived with my mother in the Passyunk Projects in South Philadelphia. I don't have many memories of my father when I was younger; however, two of my earliest memories of my dad revolves around his actions toward my mother.

I remember getting picked up by my father one day with my sisters and going to one of his friend's homes. It was dark and cold. I remember being hungry and his friend had kids that were not so nice to me. I was about three years old. I also remember the fear and concern in my mother's eyes when we returned home because, apparently, my father was never supposed to take us over there. When I got older, I found out that my father took us because he was upset that my mother was going out with her friends and asked him to watch us. He then told my grandfather that my mother had abandoned us.

My next memory came around age four or five. On some weekends, I remember visiting my father and stepmother, who had a son and daughter of her own. I remember how excited I used to be when I knew I was going to visit them. I would have my bags packed and waiting at the door with excitement, but I was often disappointed. My dad wouldn't call, nor would he show up to get us. I would cry all night, wondering what had happened. My mother tried her best to make me feel better, but the feeling of rejection was prevalent early on in my life.

Although he didn't always come when he was supposed to, my dad would call and check on me from time to time. He would ask me questions about school and how things were going. However, he never really stayed on the phone long. There were plenty of times when my mom and dad would be on the phone arguing before we got a chance to talk to him, so there was tension during the call, mostly because I didn't like seeing my mother upset, and I knew he was the one that upset her. My mother never enjoyed talking to my dad when we were around, but the walls in the projects were thin; we could still hear them. Their arguments would be about money, my dad coming to get us, or his lack of attention when he did have us. As I mentioned earlier, I loved going to visit my dad. He was there physically, but he was emotionally and spiritually unavailable. My dad would pick us up on Fridays, and from the time he picked us up until Sundays, when my mom came and got us, he would either be in his room or riding around in his car doing whatever he wanted. My stepmother took care of us. She would take us out to eat and to her job. She would let us go to the park and watch movies with us. She was great! I had good female role models between her and my mother, but I was still missing that fatherly love and attention.

I wanted to be a "daddy's girl" so bad when I was younger. I wanted my dad to play in the park with me, help me learn how to ride a bike, skate, and even beat up the boys that bothered me. But he gave off the perception that he loved himself and his women more than he loved me. And I will even take one step further because I thought he loved my stepbrother more than he loved me. He would do things with him, watch movies and shows, take him places, and then I would have to hear about it when I came over to their house. My stepbrother was even calling him dad. It was heartbreaking.

Out of all my siblings, I was the only one that worried the most about my father's absence. My mom and oldest sister would tell me not to let his choices get to me, but as a young kid, it bothered me. I remember thinking, "Am I not good enough for him?" "Does he not love me?" or "Does he love my step-siblings more than me because he lived with them?" But as I got older, I just got tired of asking those questions. I even got tired of looking for his calls and pick-ups. I became numb, so I believe I blocked out so much because I didn't want to remember the pain of neglect, rejection, and worthlessness. And what made it worst was that everyone would tell me often, "Oh my goodness, you look just like your father." "You are your father's twin." But little did they know, I hated those words as a child. Why would I want to look like someone who doesn't even feel I'm good enough to be around? So at that point, I didn't like looking in the mirror. I didn't like what I saw, and my self-esteem dimensioned quickly.

By the time I got to the third grade, I didn't like myself, and the kids at school didn't like me either. They would call me names, bully me, and hit me often. Mostly boys. I was bigger than your average kid, dark brown, and my mother tried her best to dress a "hefty" child in the '90s while raising three kids on her own with little money. Most of my clothes were handed down or bought at a goodwill store because I needed to have elastic bands in all my pants. I used to cry and beg my mother not to make me go to school, but she had to work, so I had no choice. I would get so jealous when I saw other girls' fathers come to the school because some little boy disrespected his daughter and set him straight. I didn't have that, and I was envious. There were times I told my dad about school, or my mom would tell him, but he always had to work, and I guess he never thought going to school was important enough to request a day or a morning off. I felt helpless. There was nothing left to do but start defending myself. So I began fighting in school, and even got suspended a few times, but because I was the "good kid" in school, I was never punished for my fights. This went on for many years.

Fighting made most people think I was toughing up, but I was still very weak inside. The fighting just gave me someone to take all my aggression out on. There were so many things to be angry about. My mother had just uprooted us from the only place I had ever lived and moved us to the suburbs, puberty was setting in, and to top it off, my father had left my stepmother and married another woman behind her back. Devastation, confusion, and being angry were understatements. After all these years, my dad married someone other than the woman I had loved as my stepmother. How could he do that? She was a great woman to him. I was angry, and I made sure he knew it with my silence because I couldn't fight him.

I didn't speak to my father for a while after he married this woman. I was so heartbroken. Now I was about eleven or twelve. I didn't know all the details, but I did know that he was with my stepmother and did not break up with her until after he married a new woman. I couldn't put my head around it. But soon after, he broke her heart, and I didn't get to see her as often as I would have liked. My stepbrother, my step-sister, my step-niece, Gone! Ripped away from me because he made a choice to cheat and marry someone else. My dad wanted my sisters and I to give his new wife a chance. But how could we? Our loyalty was with our stepmother, and she didn't deserve to be treated that way by him, no matter what. He would ask us to come over and get to know his wife and her children, but it felt like betrayal to me. I stood my ground and stayed loyal to my stepmother, which caused a big issue for my father and me. We continued to have a period where we didn't talk for months. He knew nothing about my life because I had so much resentment in my heart and wouldn't let him in. I didn't want to address it, nor did I want his lies and excuses about what he had done. I was going through my own battles as a preteen.

This was a crucial time in my life because I was trying to figure out who I was. My hormones were changing, and although I wasn't being bullied as much anymore, I still had difficulty creating relationships with friends. The boys started to seem interested, but I lacked confidence and had low self-esteem. I met several young ladies that were way older than me and they took me under their wings. They, too, had daddy issues, and it showed. They were already having sex, two were already mothers, and their risky behaviors screamed, "I'm without a father." I decided not to have sex like them but still indulged in risky behaviors that were not age-appropriate. I dated guys way older than me, smoked, and drank whenever my older girlfriends got a hold of some stuff. I even met guys I didn't know at their homes just for attention. I was a hurt little girl. And to make matters worse, my dad was (now) denying my sisters and me as his children, so we all had to get a DNA test.

DNA? Are you kidding me? All my life, I keep hearing how much I look like him, his mother, and his sister, and he's denying me! How could he do this to me? To my sister's? To my mother? We were all upset and furious. When the DNA test came back, my oldest sister's test showed my father was 99.9%, and mine showed that he was 99.9% our father. However, the DNA test revealed he was not the father of our youngest sister. When my mother sat us in the room to give us the news, I remember the feeling of numbness, anger, and confusion. I asked my mother why we had to get the test done, and she informed me that she requested that my father started giving her money to take care of us. We were getting older and costing her a lot more money, and she felt it was unfair to continue caring for her children alone. She said my father didn't want to pay and was upset that she took him to court, so he denied being our father. All I remember thinking was, "Wow! Rejected yet again!"

I remember crying in my bedroom so many times because of the pain caused throughout our household by someone who claimed he loved us. I was angry, so I stayed away from my father for a while. Then, he would call, and the conversations were short and sweet. I was never disrespectful to him despite what he had done. And there were even times I found myself laughing on the phone with him or talking like nothing had happened. But that was just me. The softhearted forgiving one. Both my sisters were pretty much done with him. But he knew that I had a soft spot for him in my heart. I was like putty in his hands. I cared about how he felt, and I didn't want him sad or hurt, but what was I supposed to do with my hurt? I had no clue.

The risky behaviors with boys continued because, in my mind, they helped me block the pain. They made me feel special. I was about thirteen or fourteen when I met the boy I thought was my true love. We dated for about 1 ½ years. I lost my virginity, and then he cheated. I grew angrier but didn't let that stop me from my search for love and belongingness. I needed to fill that void. I needed to be with someone. And that's when I met my high school sweetheart Jayden. We were together all through high school and my first two years of college. I never talked to my dad about boys, nor did he ask. He didn't seem interested. He would always say, "You better stay sweet for as long as you can." Little did he know that sweetness had left a long time ago.

My father may have never asked about my endeavors, but he soon found out when I was going on eighteen or nineteen when I found out I was pregnant. I was so scared to tell my dad because I had just gone off to college and was in the honors society. He was so proud. He constantly called me "his daughter with the brains and beauty." And although he disappointed me so much in life, I still didn't want to be a disappointment to him and tell him, but I had to. I expected him to get a little upset or be disappointed like some fathers would be of their daughters. However, his response was, "So you know now that you are pregnant, the state considers you an adult, and whether you're in college or not, I don't have to pay child support anymore." My heart was crushed. Child support? He really thought his little $72 every two weeks was something! "Is he really money hungry that he would say that to his child at a time like this in her life"? I was pissed, and by this time, I began to show it.

Since he loved to remind me that I was grown, I politely let him know how his heartless comment made me feel. He responded, "I was just

52

letting you know what the state was going to say." Not thinking that I knew he would have to tell the state I was pregnant; they wouldn't just know right away. But that's what he did. He told the state I was pregnant, and the payments stopped shortly after. So here we go, another case where I feel rejected and neglected. But I had to worry more about my unborn child while preparing for her arrival. I worked two jobs and went to school while pregnant. My father would call and ask why I don't call him, and most of the time we talked, it was about him. He never had a conversation with Jayden about how to treat his daughter and granddaughter. He never got upset about me being a teen mom; it just seemed like he was happy as long as I wasn't in his pockets.

Money was one thing my dad seemed to care about more than anything. It seemed to make him who he was. He was money driven. He had the best cars and clothes, and all his sneakers had to be clean and white. His appearance was everything. Never did he think about how it made us feel when he showed up looking like he stepped out of a GQ magazine while his children were wearing second-hand clothes. As long as he was well put together, he was happy. His cars were very nice.

Meanwhile, his children were riding the bus, traveling daily from one part of the city to another to get to school. I never understood how, as a man, he could allow us to struggle so much but he did. He made sure he paid his wife's bills and took great care of her, which made me so jealous because they got parts of him that I never did.

Jayden and I didn't last long after our daughter was born. He didn't want me to have her because we were "too young for a family." I was devastated. I never wanted my daughter to endure the same feelings of rejection and neglect, but she did. Jayden would go weeks without calls, just like my father. He put anything and everyone before her, just like my father did. He didn't seem to care about the things she had going on in life, just like my father did. I couldn't believe I had a baby with someone that was just like my father.

History had repeated itself. But I thought things would be different when I met and started dating a man that was fourteen years older than me named Steve. You would think my dad would have been pissed, right? Nope! He said he cared more about my happiness than our age difference. But I wanted him to care about me. I wanted him to give Steve a hard time. But, instead, he just let him have me without any fight.

Steve had no clue what to do with me. He cheated repeatedly. He was disrespectful and very mean at times. He would try to make up for his actions with gifts or make me laugh. There were times he would just act as if nothing had happened. But I wanted to be loved so bad that I stayed in an eleven-year relationship with him. I stayed with him because I wanted to feel loved, protected, and cared for. I no longer wanted to feel rejected. But I wasn't ready. I had not learned how to respect a man. I remember getting into many arguments with Steve about my lack of respect. Finally, after several relationship counselors, we realized that it was because my father wasn't an active part of my life.

I hid my toxic relationship from my dad for many years, but when I finally told him, he talked with me about not giving up on my relationship and fighting for it if I truly wanted it. Our relationship had me feeling so lost and hopeless that I began going to counseling on my own. My therapist was phenomenal. She started helping me peel back the layers of my childhood and my past. She had me complete lessons from a book by Iyanla Vanzant called "Living through the Meantime: Learning to break the patterns of the past and begin the Healing process."

The homework assignments from my therapist were getting tougher and tougher by the week. But then we hit the "father's" section of the book, and I immediately shut down. I would cry every time I would start answering questions. It was too painful to deal with. I figured, why should I keep opening that wound? I was doing fine. But I wasn't, and I needed to talk with my father.

So, one day, right before my 30th Birthday, I talked with my father. I was so nervous. I felt like that scared little girl all over again, but it had to be done. I asked him questions about his absence, his choices with women, and the reasoning behind the DNA test. My father said he didn't know how to be a father because he was never taught. He mentioned several times that he had no idea what to do with girls. He figured he was doing a good thing by getting us because some men in his era weren't even getting their children.

He got defensive when we began discussing the DNA test and how he went from woman to woman. He blamed my stepmother for his actions because she didn't want to get married. He blamed my mother for the DNA test because he said she wouldn't let him claim us on his taxes like he had always done. He said, "She was spiteful to me, so I figured I would prolong the child support by getting a DNA test done." I was furious.

You're telling me my hurt and pain were because of a petty game he wanted to play with my mother? I then began telling him how I felt about his reaction to my pregnancy and being with an older man. He couldn't understand why I was so hurt. Instead, he got quiet and shut down on me. Right after, he yelled about how my sisters and I treated my mother better than him and how we kept making him live in the past. He cried and just shut down on me. The conversation couldn't continue because he was no longer willing to talk. After that, I got no calls. I also didn't make any attempts myself. And to be even more childish, I received a text for mother's day and my Birthday. No calls. This continued until I posted something on Facebook, and one day he responded. Deep down inside, I was happy that our silence was broken, but we never revisited that conversation. I was happy with that for the moment.

I spoke to my therapist about it, and I realized that my father might not be able or willing to work through the things that occurred in our past. And that's okay. I was able to get the release that I needed for me. I could no longer allow past hurt and pain to dictate my future. I needed to heal and become whole, and although it didn't seem like the conversation resolved anything, that wasn't true. So, moving forward, I have opened up to my father and talked to him about things that bother me. I limit myself to some things because his health is declining, and I don't want to cause him any stress. But overall, I can express myself much better.

As I got older and more successful in my life, and my father's life took a turn in the wrong direction, our relationship changed. His health was declining, his marriage was failing, and all the things and people he had put before me were no longer around. He needed to lean on the one person that he hurt so badly. Me! I know he had to humble himself to ask for my help, but once he knew he had it, he made sure he used it every chance he got. A big part of me wanted to make him feel how he had made me feel all those years. I wanted to make him hurt because now he needed me. But I prayed long and hard and asked God to forgive me for even thinking that way.

I had to understand that my blessings come from God, and I did not want to block them, so whenever he needed me, I was there. I took time out of my busy schedule to assist him with the things he needed. But it didn't seem like that was good enough for him. He would still complain about me not answering my calls or attending to his needs as fast as he would have liked. But this time, we were in a much better space, and I was able to communicate with him the level of selfishness he was displaying. In addition, I was working and had children to raise during this time.

When I started to evaluate my relationship with my father in connection with our culture and his upbringing, I realized that my father loved me the best way he knew how. He wasn't taught how to be a father by his father, and in our culture, if he ever asked for help and showed any sign of weakness, then he wasn't man enough. Just because he came and got us was a big deal for him and made him feel like he was a good father. And even through all the madness and craziness, my father was at every graduation, birthday party, and family function. That was another way he showed his love was by being present and I did not realize that as I was growing up.

The little girl inside me always wishes her dad held her when she had night terrors. She will always wonder what it would feel like for her father to read her a book, and she will always wonder what it would be like to go to a daddy/daughter dance. But the truth is, I'm no longer that little girl, and I have to let go of the hurt, pain, and resentment if I want to be healed. That feeling of freedom when you have allowed something to weigh you down for many years is rewarding.

Through my healing with my father, I was able to increase my self-esteem and realize my self-worth. My dad isn't perfect, but he now tells me he loves me more. He tells me how proud he is of me for gaining not one degree but two. He checks on me often and tries to give me fatherly advice in my relationships. He was even supportive when I left Steve and told me, "I am a beautiful woman who deserves the best." My father knows he was not the perfect father; He knows that if he was a better father that our relationship would be better; He knows that he missed out on so much because of the choices he made, and because of this, I don't feel the need to remind him constantly. I have forgiven him, not just for him but for me. And although he may never say it, I know he appreciates me and my ability to forgive him.

Sakinna J.

ABOUT THE AUTHOR

SAKINNA J

Sakinna J is a #1 Best-Selling Author, Certified Transitional, and Family Life Coach, Social worker, and CEO/Founder of I Choose Me, a company that helps women regain, restore, and rebuild their lives after experiencing domestic violence.

Sakinna helps other women take back their power and live their best lives as their best selves through one-on-one coaching with her 5-step program and group coaching. She is currently working on her third anthology, where she will be a co-author in Blessed Not Broken Vol 5.

Sakinna J is a Philadelphia native who resides in Lancaster, Pennsylvania, with the love of her life and their five daughters. She attended Millersville University, receiving her B.A. in Psychology and her Master's in Social work. Sakinna is currently a member of Ebenezer Baptist Church in

Lancaster, and she enjoys spending time with her family and friends, shopping, traveling, reading, and listening to music.

Sakinna has presented on several platforms to discuss her life challenges and how she overcame them. She has been on 96.1 WURD Radio station and The Romans 12: 2 Experience radio show. She has been recognized and featured in Scoop Magazine and Black Women Mean Business Issue VI. Sakinna has also done various podcasts such as Wake, Pray Shine, The Butterfly Effect, and All Bets on Me, just to name a few.

You can connect with Sakinna J at: sakinnaj601@gmail.com, Facebook:

https://www.facebook.com/sakinna1 or Instagram: https://www.instagram.com/sakinnaj

Facebook: https://www.facebook.come/sakinna1
Instagram: https://www.instagram.com/sakinnaj

CHAPTER FIVE

My Daddy Died 4 Times: Family Secrets

BY FOCUS JAMES

At ten years old and second to the youngest in that house, I remember my play cousins and I huddled around the TV at my play Aunt's house; we were watching something I was not sure my Mom would approve of. I was torn between whether or not to say something that would spoil the fun planned for the weekend. Then, the phone rang, and I felt weird for some strange reason. I turned around and looked into my aunt's mouth. I couldn't stop staring as she said, "uh-huh, uh-huh." I knew something was wrong. She looked at me as she hung up slowly and said, "Turn around and watch the movie." I can't even tell you what happened after that. My mind raced while wondering what that call was about. How did I know it was about me? However, I felt something horrible had happened. I could not imagine what it could be.

At 8:00 am the following day, there was a knock at the door. Never before had my aunt woke me up so early in the morning. She said, "I'm going to walk you to your house…get dressed." I questioned myself, "Walk me to my house?" My aunt was the kind of person who would call one of us from downstairs to change the channel or hand her the remote control in her bedroom. Now, I was sure something was wrong. My house was only 3/4 of a block away. Usually, she would watch me walk down or, better yet, have someone watch me walk down to my house.

There were so many cars parked everywhere. I opened the door, heard people talking, and then heard muffled crying from upstairs. I turned the corner, and there was a hush in the room. My Mom said to me, "Your Dad had an aneurysm. That means something erupted in his brain, and he died." I was stunned and overwhelmed by so many people looking at me. I can now clearly hear that it's my brother crying.

Slowly I got up and backed away. I felt my brother's pain deeper with every step on the stairs. I heard my brother wailing, screaming, rolling back and forth, which was overwhelming. I listened to his bed squeaking, making so much noise. I opened the door, and tears flooded his eyes. He couldn't even see it was me. I moved a little closer, and he saw my silhouette wiping his eyes. He reached out for me to come to him. He pulled me onto his bed and rocked me back and forth, screaming and wailing. I don't even remember how I got away from his clutches. It was all a blur.

Sadly, I could not feel the depth of his pain. I barely knew our Daddy. I only had three memories of him.

One memory is from when I was around five or so. My Daddy and Mom were in the foyer holding each other in a headlock and punching each other's faces. They both were bleeding, or there was blood on both their faces. That's all I got for that memory.

My second memory is when I was around eight. My father came to take my middle brother and me to the movies. I remember looking back, and my mother looked terrified as we walked away to catch the bus. The movie was great, and my Dad got me a Teddy Bear. I cherish that time with my Daddy.

My third memory is just a few days before my Daddy died. (Unbeknownst to me, My Daddy was just released from jail for domestic abuse, which I would not find out until I was in my twenties). He arrived at our home,

BANGING on the steel door that opened outward that was installed by Women Against Abuse. It was a safety precaution.

The door swung open, causing the person on the steps to back down, then step back up to come inside. The house felt like it was rocking, and the foundation was loose, which said a lot because the #47 City Transit Bus rumbled down our block every 22 minutes, shaking the entire house. We sat on the floor in the hallway. We did not want to be in front of the windows.

My Mom was fierce, and she never backed down from anyone. However, at that moment, I saw fear in her eyes to the point that I could not speak. She told my brother and me not to speak (using the universal sign, shaking her finger) over her trembling mouth. We sat there until he stopped banging. At least another hour passed, which felt like an eternity. We sat in complete silence until my Mom gave us the sign to go upstairs. I packed a bag to go to my play aunt's house to spend the entire weekend there. That was a treat because it was usually just for one night. That was the night my aunt got the call. Somehow, I knew the call was about me.

At sixteen years old, sitting in that same bed that my brother pulled me into as he rocked back and forth, wailing because of the loss of my Dad, I was now sad and depressed. My brother moved out and got married. Our middle brother was in college. My mother walked by my bedroom door and saw me throw the only thing my Dad gave me, which was My Teddy Bear with cinnamon fur and big marble eyes with pretty brown irises, like me and my Daddy's eyes. I slept with my Teddy Bear ever since my Dad gave it to me during the one memory of us spending time together.

However, that event no longer sustained me. Desperate to know how to be accepted? How to date boys? And how to fit in? I longed for my father to be able to tell me, teach me and be here to protect me. I was so sad now that I was visiting classmates' homes who had fathers. Our coach was one of my basketball teammate's Daddy. I was so envious of their relationship. The girl always seemed angry with her Dad. But I would have been so happy to have a dad to be angry with.

It was very unusual for me to be in bed past 9 am. Finally, it was around noon, so my Mom called my oldest brother. He came down to talk to me and began to share. "God will be your father. He could be your covering. Although people are saying our father committed suicide. I don't believe it." My eyes widened, and my heart sank. "I never heard that before; wait, what? He didn't have an aneurysm?"

I was so angry. As my brother's lips moved, I went into my head, but I could not hear anything else he said. Daddy chose to leave me here by myself! It's one thing that he died abruptly and just left me here. I was wrestling with how much my Daddy had control over that, or it was just his time. Since I was his daughter, could I die of an aneurysm?

I turned to sports, basketball, volleyball, softball, and ran track. I was known for going the extra mile, diving for the ball, and running harder than necessary. Because of my thoughts, I could die at any moment. Since my father had something explode in his head and he just dropped dead, couldn't I? I was pretty reckless, but it paid off. I earned sixty-three trophies, medals, and letters for my athleticism. My eldest brother earned forty-plus trophies, and my middle brother earned fifty-plus. I thought to myself, I won, but did I?

I recall explicitly walking in the hallway of my high school and seeing four girls about to jump one girl. I told them, "Not today! You wanna each fight her one at a time, go ahead, but whatcha NOT going to do, is jump her." She and I were both outnumbered. She was offended and was like, "Who are you?" I said, "Me? I'm the person that's going to stop you from getting your ass whipped."

At times, I was pretty reckless with my behavior. "Because at any moment, I could drop dead, too." But hearing this news of the possibility of my

Daddy committing suicide. I was grieving all over again that this bastard would choose to leave me here alone. I was dealing with everything my Mom had to deal with, from her outbursts, upset, and depression to her grief. It was squeezing the life out of me, and you are telling me that this man chose to leave me. I was brokenhearted all over again.

The next day, I went to church with my brother. This decision radically changed my life within months. I was groomed to choose between the few single men in the church. I was told that only a few good men would be arriving. I'd better pick before I didn't have any. I found myself being part of multiple committees, organizations, and auxiliaries to keep busy so the devil won't use my idol mind.

The school year was ending. I broke up with this beautiful young man who stood 6'9" tall. He played on our rival school basketball team because he was "not saved." It hurt so much that I needed to give him up in the name of Jesus. By the next school year, I was no longer wearing pants and quit all of my athletic activities. The doctrine taught that it was not of God for me to wear pants; therefore, I needed to stop sports.

At seventeen, I came back to school, telling everyone I was engaged, and I wasn't going to college. My soon-to-be husband forbids me to go to college because he wouldn't date anyone long-distance. So, it was quite a shock to see me, TJ, who wore pants every day with sneakers and a ponytail, now wearing my hair out with curls and long skirts. Everyone was shocked, including me.

I didn't know how to adjust and have regular conversations. Everything had to begin and end with God. I became very dogmatic in my speech. I was pushing all my friends away. All in the name of God, and Jesus is my savior. I was looking to escape from the pain of my Mom still dealing with my Dad's death.

And to make matters worse, now my Mom was angry at my brother for getting me to be a part of what she said was a "cult." I had to escape.

What better way than to marry a Christian who wants me to be a homemaker and be barefoot and pregnant in the kitchen? Sounds pretty ideal. Except I was very ambitious. I wanted to own multiple daycare centers. I wanted to go to Virginia State to play volleyball. I wanted to have a whole life. At this church, we weren't allowed to wear pants or play sports or even go to the movies, nor could we wear makeup or jewelry. If they had their way, we wouldn't even have a perm.

When I returned to school after the summer with an engagement ring, the news traveled fast. "Ms. James, please report to Mrs. King's classroom," blared over the PA system. I slowly walked to Mrs. King's class and peeked my head in her door. No one was there. I sat down, and a few minutes later, Mrs. King walked in, slammed down sheets of paper, and said, "Complete the application."

The scholarship application had the same surname as Mrs. King. "The King Scholarship." I was one of her favorite students. I was already doing college math. She couldn't fathom me NOT going to college and was angry. She would barely speak to me and be very brief from that day forward. No longer did I receive resounding accolades for how well I was doing. It was a sharp, quick, good job. I had lost so much becoming a Christian to get what I missed from my Daddy: My friends, all of my sports, and even my favorite teacher. However, all in the name of Jesus and having a sense of belonging and obeying God, it was a small price to pay, right?

I found myself in a serious relationship before the age of twenty. I'm still looking for that covering, belonging, and validation not received from my Daddy. It was a tumultuous relationship. Loving God is not enough. We must #healthehurt, or we will repeat the pain. Also, we need to know how to problem-solve, communicate with the opposite sex, and know ourselves to choose a soulmate for life. At our young ages, neither one of us knew ourselves.

Doctors told me I would never have children during the first month of our relationship because I have Polycystic Ovaries Syndrome. My husband and mother fasted and prayed over me. Two months after being married, I was pregnant. A baby was carrying a baby. I was overwhelmed by the thought of "How is this baby going to come (turn) OUT."

Plus, I was in college via a scholarship at Community College, thanks to Mrs. King. It was so hard on my small-framed body carrying the baby for nine months. I gained fifty pounds and could not see it on me. The tech could not find the baby's heartbeat at my biweekly appointment. They took me to another floor in the hospital to use a more "in-depth machine" to find (revive) the baby's heartbeat. In other words, "get me away from the other mothers." We lost the baby. I was blamed because there were constant arguments during the first year of our relationship. Both of us were screaming, hollering, and even a few scuffles. I attempted to console him, but he was not accepting my efforts. He was bitter toward me for a long time, and our relationship was never the same.

At my young age, I was able to have a child. They were not letting up, as he was one of several children from an extremely large family. Next, he became a preacher. I was very proud and admired his way of putting a sermon together. Shortly after, he received an offer to become a pastor. Our high church official disagreed and recommended we needed way more time to go through the process of becoming a pastor. I agreed. I knew we didn't need to leave. I needed a safe, secure place to continue to grow our relationship, which was looking pretty bleak. I desperately pleaded with him, saying we were not ready to go. I was frowned upon once again as if the devil was using me. He then became the junior pastor of the church, and my responsibilities increased dramatically.

I was saddened to leave our home church. I knew I wasn't ready for that level of responsibility in my twenties with a small child and people staring at me like I was in a fishbowl. I wanted no part of it. He began leaving the house every night for some reason regarding God, the church, and the people. I told him I didn't get into a relationship to feel like I was single. He said God comes first. So don't let the devil use you.

That's pretty much how all of our conversations went. He was more educated and indoctrinated around the Bible. So, anything I said, he had several scriptures to back him up to prove that the devil was using me and he was doing God's work as head of the house.

I remember explicitly one day. I was watching TV, and he walked into the house. He snatched the remote out of my hand and put it on top of the TV. As he turned it off, he said, "Oprah, she's a snake. You will not be watching Oprah on my TV in my house." He turned around and went up the steps.

I remember tears streaming down my face. And I said to myself, what did I get myself into? I thought I was leaving a WOUNDED relationship for a HEALED person. I thought I left a person who constantly lashed out at me 'because there was no one else home' because they hadn't dealt with the hurt and pain of losing their relationship to tragedy. Instead, I just picked my Mom in a different form. This is even worse because this is someone I'm expected to care for, cook, clean, understand, listen to, follow, and have sex with.

He began to forbid me from going to church. Then, he started making excuses about why I needed to stay home. I was moving too slow, etc.

We were now separated. He came from his sister's house to talk to me one day. Furious with anger and disgust, he said, "I don't love you anymore, and the relationship is over, dead. I want to live a life unto Christ and preach the word of God. But I am stopped because I only have one wife!" He smacks the table, shaking the entire room. I jump up in silence and back up to the wall. He approached me nose to nose, telling me this marriage was of the devil and God ain't in you, so you might as well commit suicide like your father did to free you and me."

His craziness went on and on as he smacked the wall screaming and grinding his teeth as if he was going to hit me. Terrified in silence, I just stood there. Once again, he told me to commit suicide. He stormed away and slammed the door shaking the house. I slid down the wall and cried silently until the sun went down. Finally, while getting up, I recognized that I did not escape from the pain of my past. It was all right here. Too scared of pain, I vowed I would not hurt myself and leave my child behind to feel the pain I felt from my Dad committing suicide.

The Truth will seek you out. Brace yourself to receive it and flow with it.

As time went on, I still lived my life as a woman in a relationship. I dare not tell anyone of our separation. I was devastated! I continued going to work and coming home, not going to anyone's church because they would know my unwanted secret.

One evening, a dear friend called me and said, "Hey, what are you doing?" I said, "nothing." She said, "Let's take a ride?" I said, "sure." No one had been reaching out to me. It was as if I was in isolation, tabooed. I was also confused by the distance I felt, starting with my husband's church members and my old church members. I was happy to have the company, and when she arrived, I jumped in the car and started chatting while driving.

I looked up as she was pulling over. I said, "Why are we here at his church? She said, "Just get out and take a look." I got out of the car and looked in the storefront window of our church. His parents were in the pulpit, which was normal. Our nanny, the armor-bearer for the pastor and Junior pastor, was noticeable. She was also standing beside him. I realized they were dressed alike; my husband wore a Navy-blue suit with a Paisley tie. She was wearing a Navy-blue dress with a matching scarf.

They dipped into each other's ears while talking. He touched the lower part of her back with an embrace. I broke down and cried. Oh my God, the church is packed. It's a revival. And they're all watching and participating, knowing they are having an affair. Our nanny was acting like she was the First Lady. I ran to the car, hoping no one saw me.

I cried until I couldn't cry anymore. I had no tears left when we got back to my house. My tears, throat, and face were burning from the deep breaths I was trying to take to catch my breath. I went into our home alone that night and cried myself to sleep. I mind-mapped about all the times that now made sense concerning their interactions.

I traveled out of state with my old church to a revival. Now I realized why everyone was so distant. They knew he was cheating. He was sat down (as a church leader) but only after my Mom called the Bishop and demanded action. A family member met me at the revival.

We talked it up for about five minutes back at the hotel when they began to tell me, "I gotta tell you something. My father did NOT commit suicide. Someone killed him, and I know who." "Wait, what did you say? So, he didn't have an aneurysm? He didn't commit suicide." Absolutely not, because I know, because I was there. When I arrived, he was already dead. At this point, I'm enraged that he (my father) didn't just up and die from an aneurysm. He didn't kill himself and leave me. Someone took him away from me.

And the grieving process began again. I was enraged that people knew who did it and didn't do anything about it. My whole life was altered because of someone else's indiscretion. Is that fair? I grew angry at people of authority. I grew mad at people anytime I felt like there was an injustice. And on command and on-demand, I was there to save the weak and balance the injustice done to me. Since someone took my father away, having no peace and no rest, I constantly looked for ways to equalize their fault. I was always in distress, filled with stress, and misunderstood.

By my late twenties, I had my own apartment. However, we had not severed our financial affairs because I refused to sign the financial paperwork even after he had twins with the nanny. As a result, I was scared to be alone and move on with the rest of my life.

The Truth will seek you out. Brace yourself to receive it and flow with it.

Now, in my early thirties, I received a visit from a family member who wanted to get the proper markings for my father's grave. In addition, he was asking for donations to pay for it.

"Listen, please, can you tell me the Truth? What happened? How did he (my father) die? I just want the Truth."

"Well, your father had been raping that family member since she was a child. Once he got into her house, this time, it wasn't going to happen the way it had happened many times before. But, yes, he tried to rape her. She had a very rough life. And she shot him in defense. It was not only her; he attempted to rape several other family members. And your mother feared that he would try to rape you. And that's why you all had to leave the house and stay with family and women & children's shelters."

Wait, what? My father did not commit suicide because now we have someone else holding the gun. Nor was he murdered. He was a rapist to family members, and he was killed by one of his victims. I was beyond exasperated. Distraught that my father was a rapist. I was troubled that my family members had to go through being raped by someone they knew.

Why would my Mom still have that monument of him in the living room? "As if he was the best dad ever," I wondered how she could revere him the way she does. She never said a bad word about him to us. My Mom would always say," he was never right after the car accident." I couldn't dare tell her that I knew.

What was I supposed to do with this information? My father, a rapist? I've read about rapists and watched movies about rapists. I feared rapists. And my father, who brought me into this world, raped women, several women. My God, what if he had raped me? Psychologically, what and who would I be?

Wait, what about my family members? I began to run my mental tapes back, remembering different things said and done. Then, finally, I remembered the family member who had behavioral health issues. That was one of the people he raped. I couldn't bear the thought that she was the way she was because of what he had done to her.

I began calling different organizations centered around sexual assault victims and shared with them that my father was a rapist and that he raped several of our family members. I don't know what to do. Is there a support group for me, being his daughter, knowing what he did? I made call after call, and there was none. You see, the rapist has no voice. Nor the family members that were scarred by the rapist's actions. Somber, confused, feeling guilty, and powerless.

I sunk deeper into work, ambition, achieving, succeeding, and believing that I was going to do better in the world. I was going to use my degrees in Early Childhood Education and Communication, Broadcast Theater, and Mass Media to understand humanity and Create Juicy Love.

It took me ten years to #healththehurt of my father's death and the betrayal of a lover having outside babies. I traveled to thirty-seven states, going to workshops, seminars, and business leadership conferences to transform my spirit.

And today, I helped thousands of others to do #healththehurt. While writing this chapter, it's my third anniversary of having my Love&Life and Business Coaching Practice full time. I created a program to help the most profound hurt transform into Healed Hurt, which equals Purpose.

Also, while writing this chapter, I was invited to come on stage with "THE" Tony Robins at the Virtual Unlimited Breakthrough Event. So, after sharing my story and evolution with him, here's how I will end this tragic saga that gave birth to my PURPOSE, TheFocusoflove.com, with Tony's amazing Summary of it all:

"When you can take the worst experiences of your life and then solve them, then you have a gift you can give others. Then you have a gift that you can give others that everybody can't give because you have an experience that some people intellectually know, but you know experientially.

"You went through a different kind of pain; you went through a spiritual pain. Spiritual pain is different than just physical pain. I'm sure you have physical pain as well, but spiritual pain is when the person that loves you most or you love the most tries to harm you. When you go through spiritual pain, you end up with spiritual power because the power is when you can heal that.

That is a whole different level. That makes you someone who could help others heal because you actually live it. You aren't talking about it with words. You haven't read it in a book; you've experienced it. So, I don't even know the concept of what you're doing, but I'm sure it's incredibly effective because you lived it. I loved that you did that. And really honor you for that. Give her a hand for that. I love that you took a problem and turned it into a gift" Tony Robins to Focus at Unlimited Breakthrough.

I invite you to Heal your spirit and your daddy wounds by going to TheFocusOfLove.com and schedule a Discovery Zoom Session with me, Focus James, so you don't have to suffer in silence anymore. You are not alone! See you on Zoom.

Coach Focus James
#healthehurt

ABOUT THE AUTHOR

FOCUS JAMES

Since her playground days in elementary school, Focus has been speaking up for the underdog. Throughout the years, her passion for the growth and development of children and young adults compelled her to earn a degree in Early Childhood Education. With her passion, education, and experience, Focus can speak to the little girl or boy inside each of us. She furthers her education by receiving a degree in Communications, Theater, Broadcast, and Journalism. This led her to become a Master of Communication and enhanced her ability to hear beyond spoken words. Focus has the uncanny ability to inspire, motivate and empower others while breathing life into untold stories.

Her latest accomplishment is co-authoring with nine other authors in "Harness The Power of Purpose: How to Monetize Your Personal And Business Journey"! Focus earned a certification as a transformational life coach, teacher, trainer, and speaker from the world-renowned John C. Maxwell team. The John C. Maxwell organization is the #1 producer of leaders and coaches worldwide. Additionally, she has received a Speaker's Certificate awarded by Inspire2Speak, a speaker's camp created and founded by Dr. James Dentley, with special guest presenter, master motivator, and storyteller Les Brown. Focus' first book is titled "What is The Focus Of Love." A book stocked full of breakthroughs and aha moments for you to have.

With her extensive training in coaching and leadership, dynamic and engaging speaking abilities, compassion, and drive, Focus will help you propel your life forward to your desired destination. With Focus as your coach, teacher, and trainer, you will be able to have the life you love and gain the ability to create the skills needed to live on your highest frequency and build core beliefs and habits that serve your highest being. With her dynamic curriculum, your organization will be astonished at its own abilities to achieve what you've been longing to do! Let the journey begin!

Testimonial:

"We would not be Married NOW if it was not for Focus & God! First, Focus helped my husband have a breakthrough within himself during the pandemic to even find me. After dating and getting engaged, Focus recommended developing a beautiful company together to create synergy as a couple. We came up with six phenomenal opportunities. First, we agreed to start with our Youtube Channel since we are in a pandemic. The "Hangin with The Howards" Youtube Channel featured our wedding. Second, being newlyweds is hard, and without meeting with Focus every Monday from 8:30-930 to build our Love and Legacy, we would have given up. Third, marriage just was not the fallacy of social media. The media and influencers said it was, and we didn't know what a healthy marriage looked like since neither of us had that example. Thank you, Focus, for strategically educating us on the tools to communicate and understand ourselves as individuals, each other, and how to function as a married couple. We believe all couples and particularly Newlyweds need Focus."

Fatimah and Lavon Howard
Ms. Focus James
Company Name/Title: The Focus Of Love LLC
Contact: 2679781247
Website: www.focusjames.com
email: focus@focusjames.com

Social Media:
https://www.facebook.com/focus.james.3/
https://www.instagram.com/thefocusoflove/

CHAPTER SIX

A Father To The Fatherless

BY BEVERLY LARUE

After being asked to be a part of the Daddy Daughter Dynamic book project, I had mixed emotions. I started thinking that I can't be a Daddyless daughter because my father was physically in my life. As my emotions faded as I looked back over my life through my interactions with my father, only to realize I was a Daddyless daughter in some areas of my life.

Growing up, I would love to see a little girl holding her Daddy's hand. I sensed the strength and security that fathers provided in that small jester. I would have a lingering smile that touched my heart long after the image. It gave me a warm feeling in my soul.

I know this is a typical everyday image for some people, a Daddy holding his daughter in his arms and close to his heart. I would stare when I saw a father holding his daughter's hand because it meant so much more to me. My heart would feel the bond of their love. I'd try not to stare, but the joy in my heart wanted to capture that image and save it. Likewise, hearing stories of Daddies taking their daughters out to dinner and showing her she's a queen has great value and meant so much to me as a little girl, teenager, young adult, and, yes, a mature woman!

Another image that touches my heart is a Daddy and Daughter in conversation, laughing and talking. The father shares his wisdom about life and boys with their young daughter. Finally, he closes their conversation by saying, daughter, I hope you understood everything I've said. Now always remember, I'm here for you whenever you need me. So don't hesitate to reach out. I'm never too busy.

To see a father embrace his daughter with a loving hug of approval is empowerment. My heart would soften to see such a glorious image. And to see a daughter finishing a race and hear her father's shouts, saying; you can make it. You got this!

The Lord was so creative when he was orchestrating my healing. This lack that I felt for so many years at different stages of my life was His divine way of telling me that my heart and soul needed healing. Things happened in my life, and my mind comprehended their effects. My heart and soul needed healing, and I didn't even know. I needed a transformational breakthrough!

During my forties, my heart was still shedding layers of my emotional bandage filled with wounds of unawareness. My unawareness was the images of fathers and daughters bonding. I did not realize that the longing in my heart was the bandages of the years of curiosity about my father-daughter relationship. These uncomfortable thoughts and feelings were ready to be healed. How confusing it was, yet now I understand. This is very important to me. The word fatherless seems so cruel to both the father and the daughter. The world may associate the word fatherless with negative connotations.

Negative thoughts of pain, sorrow, disappointment, abuse, neglect, and abandonment begin to swirl around in the daughter's mind. These thoughts may devalue and belittle the father and minimize and berate any positive effort the father has shown in his role. The world will give me legitimate reasons and rights to hold on to my pain and sorrow. But God gave me the main reason to let go, forgive, and be healed for my father and me. Some of the ways I began to understand healing for my father were through his life circumstances, upbringing, experiences, hurt, and lack. For my healing to begin, my relationship needs to be present through the spiritual eyes of Father God. Spiritually a man that is a father that has less of God in him is fatherless.

He (man) can only be a father at the level that he has God in him. Therefore, He can't properly function in his God-given role as an earthly father at his highest level. Therefore, spiritually, he can't give his daughter divine support, guidance, and most of all, love.

After receiving his meaning of fatherless in my heart, I already felt the compassion for my father flood my soul. Now hearing the word fatherless makes me focus on the God of my Father. Who continually heals and restores me because his love for me is real! So now, when I think of the word fatherless, I have love and compassion for my earthly father and me.

I know in my heart there were times in my life I had less of God in me. It makes a big difference in every area of my life and relationships. We both needed healing. As a result of healing, neither one (of us) would have less of God in us. Only the overflowing presence of Father God will fill my heart and allow me to soar above every hurdle in my life.

Growing up, having my father at home was good, but having a relationship with him would have been better. It would have left me with years of childhood memories filled with father-daughter quality time. In addition to years of many conversations where he'd share his wisdom and encourage me to reach my goals, I could have learned so much more.

But most of all, he could have guided me through life's many turns, traps, and pitfalls. This book is an answered prayer of mine in my heart, which was, "Lord, I want to be made whole and complete in YOU. Please heal me." Sharing my story is part of my healing journey, wholeness, and completion through my Father God.

The first thing that helped me on my healing journey was allowing God to heal me the way he wanted to. I surrendered any idea of dealing with my earthly father-daughter issues as I cast my cares to the Lord and left them there. My healing was in the Lord's time. He divinely orchestrated events in my life to open my heart to feel pain and disappointment. Then, God's healing power would overtake me in whatever way I needed at that moment.

Sometimes I would cry while journaling my spiritual healing. But most of all, I used prayer along with worshiping God, my heavenly father. Arms that I had never felt around me drew me closer to the arms of my heavenly father. During my first healing encounter, the universe shined the light by revealing God's grace (to me) about my earthly father. God knew my father's heart better than he knew his own heart.

Another part of my healing was learning about my generation from birth. As an adult, I had to understand more about the era I grew up in. Fatherhood back then meant taking care of your family by working and providing for them. That was the father's way of showing their love for their family. With that understanding, my father loved and cared for me the best way he could. And my father always gave me his best. The best way that he showed me that he loved me was by making the decision daily to stay with my family.

Another part about my father was that he enjoyed life. He enjoyed seeing others enjoy life, including his family and friends. Having his family and friends around talking was important to him. Not only that, but he also loved to go out of town, and he always took his family with him. He could have left us at home, but he always wanted us with him. Even some of my friends looked to my father as their father figure. When they speak of my father, they tell stories of the way he taught them things and shared life nuggets with everyone. Of course, he didn't have to, but that's who my father was. Even during his fatherlessness, he shared what he had with others.

My earthly father was a good provider of security and protection. He was a hard worker who loved his family. So when I began to see my earthly Father through God's eyes of compassion, it eased the pain in my heart. Early in my father's life, he had a relationship with the Lord. He attended church and was a member of a gospel singing group.

After seeing a Pastor friend do worldly things outside the church. It was hard for him to receive the word from him. And this affected my father's relationship with the Lord. So even though my father started his life full of Father God, this incident made him feel less of God in him.

I kept remembering what the Lord revealed to me, that my earthly father, with less of God in him, makes him fatherless. That was such a revelation to me. At that very moment, I focused on God's presence in my father's life rather than on the lack of my father's parenting skills. My heart began to fill with compassion and divine understanding for my earthly father. As a little girl, my father would always say, "I pay the cost to be the boss." As a child, I never really understood what he meant. Years later, as an adult, I learned what he meant.

Every day my earthly father would get up and go to work regardless of the weather, his back pain, and the many pressures of life. He paid the costly price daily with his body to carry the whole load, so we didn't have to. My earthly father enjoyed the outdoors. I remember him sitting in the backyard for hours, just looking around and relaxing.

Early in my healing journey, the Lord revealed that while my father was sitting outside, he would talk to him and pray because he didn't go to church with the family. I thought he didn't have a relationship with the Lord. My heavenly father met my earthly father right where he was. My earthly father wasn't as full of my heavenly father as he was while starting as a young father. But even during his fatherless state, he communed with his heavenly father.

One missed childhood memory was not experiencing hugs from my earthly father. How did I let something so important slip throughout my childhood? Then, in one of my divine healing encounters, my heart began to ache, and my eyes shed tears after finally releasing the pain from a hug I would never receive.

Knowing why my father didn't hug me was very saddening, even as I thought about how he must have felt. Yet his history gave me a greater understanding of him as my father. I might not have received a physical hug from my father, but I know he loved me dearly. It's not so much the missed hugs that the Lord wanted me to experience; it's the pain and sorrow connected to it, knowing I would one day feel. He didn't want me bound by my past feelings.

Another memory of wanting to bond with my father was during my preteen years. I would go outside to the garage when he worked on the car. He enjoyed working on cars and showing other people how to fix them. Sometimes, I would go out to the garage to be around my father. We didn't say much; being in his presence was good enough for me. When he would ask me to hand him a much-needed tool, I felt like I was a part of whatever he was doing. It was as if I needed that time with my earthly father. Just being in my father's presence made me feel close to him. Father-daughter bonding can come in many ways, and this was mine.

In my mid-twenties, during my father's season of final transitioning, my father was back where he started as a young man being a father full of the presence of God. When visiting him, he would talk about the Lord. I would hear him repeatedly say, thank you, Lord. His face was full of the peace of God. Nothing seemed to matter. It was as if he cast all his cares to the Lord. He would still walk outside and sit outdoors. But now I know what he was doing.

He endured the physical pain from working as a young father now. Now, he endured his sickness as a seasoned father. Yet, even in all my

81

father's pain, I still saw his strength. The fullness of God in my earthly father's life was present in his interactions and words.

I visited my father on this divine occasion, and the whole family praised the Lord. That day, my father received the Holy Ghost. The awesomeness of seeing and hearing my earthly father talking to his heavenly father in his sacred language. I'll never forget that day. My heart overflowed with joy for my father, and we both felt the presence of our Father God at the same time.

Deep down within my heart, nothing that I have ever been through in life with my father could ever take away from his priceless value (to me) and the love that I have in my heart for him. He will always be my father, my hero. I love you, Dad.

A few years ago, the Lord dealt with me about *Jeremiah 8:22 KJV – "Is there no balm in Gilead; is there no physician there?* Why is not the health of the daughter of my people recovered?" I received the message in my heart, but I thought it was a message for other women to be healed. Not realizing my heavenly father was preparing me for my healing journey.

The heavenly father gave me subtle signs concerning my healing that I thought were scriptures to learn more about his love for me. So I know that my healing is part of his love for me.

Jeremiah 8:11 KJV – "For they have healed the hurt of the daughter of my people slightly.

This scripture led me to think that I wasn't healed. In my mind and body, I felt healed. But my heavenly father knows what it would take to heal every area of my life. While reading this scripture, I knew in my heart more healing was necessary. Sometimes I wasn't welcoming my healing because that meant I had to feel the pain again.

I am not comparing my earthly father's traits or life to my heavenly father. So likewise, there is no comparison between anyone on this earth to the true and living God. This is just how the Lord dealt with me on my healing journey.

My Heavenly Father wanted me to know that he understands fatherlessness. His fatherlessness was far greater than mine, yet he did not minimize my pain. Instead, he steered my gaze unto HIM instead of my earthly father. His father turned away from him on the cross not because of his sins but because of my sins.

This is the scripture he gave me, *Psalm 68:5 KJV – "A father to the fatherless."* This scripture let me know that Jesus was with me during my situation. He is in his role as a father to me, and he has not left me. And *Isaiah 53:3, KJV – "He is despised and rejected of men; a man of sorrow and acquainted with grief."*

My heavenly father told me first that he was a human man with feelings. And that he understood my pain, sorrow, and grief. To be acquainted with something, you must know about it because you learned it or experienced it. That scripture helped me so much. It made my healing more effortless and bearable, knowing God, my heavenly father sits on the throne. So, Jesus, his son, connects to my situation and circumstance, even if it was for a short time.

During my prayer time, Jesus gave me the example of him through his death on the cross for me. He shared this with me; He experienced fatherlessness while on the cross for us. He is acquainted with a father not being there in our darkest hour. The pain, disappointment, sorrow, and tears fell like blood. The heartache of feeling loneliness and the anguish from the pain breaks a daughter's heart when a father is absent. A sudden absence leaves him asking Father, Father, why have you forsaken me? Even though it was only three days, it felt like an eternity. The thought of my father turning away from me hurt.

I went through this act of love for you, my daughter so that you can have a relationship with my Father God. Going through the pit of hell and getting the keys to death was horrible. Not having my father protect and guide me was forever etched in my mind and heart. But Jesus understood the necessary guidance needed in my life.

I received abuse and torture at the hands of the very people my heavenly father sent me to. Instead, the people who were supposed to accept and love me, wronged me. Although they seemed to want me around at times, they devised plans to abuse and neglect me. From the many beatings to spitting on me and the agonizing pain from plucking my beard. Not to mention beating my flesh until my skin came off. I went publicly naked and unashamed, and the stares from people looking at me as if they wanted more pain inflicted on me. A pain they could never survive.

Not to mention the nails, oh, the nails. Remember that I was human, just as you are. Can you imagine how it felt to my flesh and bones with each bow of that hammer? It was as if my body was hollering through every one of my cells to stop. I felt more pain, more agony, then another nail and another. My voice is faint, and the blood floods my organs, making speech labored and breathing difficult.

I was already left without strength from carrying that heavy wooden cross. I felt lifeless at times from being flogged. I was falling under the weight of a tree my father created for his glory. That tree is being used as a spectacle against his beloved son. Yet, he allowed being birthed into humanity, the same humanity I came to save and restore their relationship with my father forever in eternity.

While carrying that heavy cross, each step felt like my knees would bust, and my ankles would break due to the severity of the beating. Those that knew me looked at me as if not to recognize me. My friends and followers looked at me with disbelief in their hearts that this whole ordeal was happening. Pain covered my mother's face, and her tears stained the road covered with my blood.

The dear mother that my heavenly father gave me to love and care for couldn't help me. The soldiers were determined that I carry my cross until they made someone standing in the crowd help me carry the cross, as everyone watched in horror. The soldiers demanded that he help me carry the cross. I'll never forget his face while we looked eye to eye, wondering. Because I knew his thoughts, "Why sis, did they beat him so bad? He shared his strength with me, and with his help, every one of my steps was a little more bearable." Being born into humanity has feelings.

I understood all too well (fatherlessness) for a moment. The feeling of disappointment, pain, shame, and hurt was evident. But, most of all, I felt a void of my father's presence in my life. While my head hung and they pierced my side, I was thinking, Father, please help me. Then they offered me sour vinegar to the lips that blessed and healed them with my heavenly father's words—forgetting these lips that told them that my father would always love them. That day, the earth shook due to the dreadfulness of the evil towards the heavenly father's son.

Now, feeling fatherless, I looked up, and with my breath, I told my father to forgive them, for they know not what they do. Forgive those who hurt your son. Forgive each person's hands that hurt me. Each person that rallied to see me crucified; forgive them because your love is in me, and your mercy and grace are for everyone. I asked my father to forgive them, for they know not what they do. My purpose in life and death could not be complete without forgiveness from the heart.

After that, I forgave my father for everything. By forgiving my father from a secure place in my heart, it was heard by my heavenly Father God that forgave me. When I forgive, just as Jesus did, I can say it's over. Forgiveness seen through the heavenly father's eyes makes it available for both the father and the daughter. So forgive your earthly father, let go of the pain, and be healed in Jesus' name. Say it is finished today" in Jesus' name. A father to the fatherless – Psalm 68:3 KJV. What about this? What do you think?

In 2007 my mother and I heard the call to start a women's book ministry. After years of meeting together, the Lord gave me the name of the book ministry. He said WOEE. The first thought that came to my mind was that whenever woe is mentioned in the bible, the Lord was trying to get my attention to avoid misfortune.

But this is what he told me. WOEE is because the women in this ministry will have been through "EXTREME THINGS IN THEIR LIVES BUT WILL BE EXCELLENT UNTO HIM." I couldn't wait to share it with the other women. He then gave me the symbol he saw for his daughters. The image I saw was a pregnant woman with a crown in her stomach and the fire of God over her head. She was pregnant with the word of the Lord and could only be birthed through spiritual midwives. She would give birth to everything God put in her.

In 2012, I was brutally attacked and beaten. That experience was very traumatic for me. I was devastated and ashamed and felt broken and damaged. My road to recovery was slow, long, and challenging. I felt fragile from the pain I endured. Yet, I could not have made it through without God's hand in my life and my family's support.

I had to rely on my family at different times, and they were always there for me. Many of my relatives and friends supported me with prayers and personal visits. My children saw their mother standing strong. And at this moment, I was in a fragile state. I had to be very gentle with myself, allowing myself to take in everything. I remember this; the attack was on a Monday, and we had women's book ministry on Tuesday.

Even in my condition, I walked with a cane while still bruised and full of wrecking pain, with several body parts wrapped in bandages. I told myself I must still do what God called me to do. Even if I don't stay at the book ministry meeting long, I must show up. Then, as I walked in using my cane, I heard someone say, "I came to see a miracle. Beverly is coming. I knew she would show up."

I knew what I was doing for God, but I did not realize that other people watched my life this closely. I had to prove that my GOD was still sitting on the throne, taking care of me. And I was still about my Father God's business despite my current life circumstance.

Even though this was very traumatic and devastating, I asked the Lord to heal me and be made whole. I was clear about being healed; at the time, I didn't know what I was asking. But I was sincere, and my words were coming from my heart. I know I wanted my life to be changed. I wanted more of what God had for me.

A few months later, I began my transformational awakening (close encounter) with the Lord that changed my life. At the beginning of my transformation, the Lord spoke these words to me. "This right here is about life or death; you choose." At that time, I stopped every plan I scheduled with my family and listened to the instructions from the Lord. I didn't know what was involved, but I knew the Lord was not playing with me.

I surrendered my will to God immediately. He was loving but firm and addressed every area of my life through a spiritual midwife. He would wake me early for days and nights and stay up late to show me my heart. He wanted to deal with the issues of my heart. Then he dealt with me about my secrets.

Even though Jesus knows everything about us, there are some things he wants us to tell him so the enemy can't hold it over our heads when Jesus calls upon us. This way, the enemy can't have a foothold in my life because I told the Lord all my secrets, and he forgave me. Do you know that the greatest secret I told the Lord gave me the greatest freedom? I was so glad the Lord loved me so much that he wanted to clean every area of my life. That brought so much healing to my soul.

That transformation of my heart felt like I was on a divine operating table. I felt the pain of the sacred instruments whose hands were firm and filled with love. My heart was open to the Lord. During this transformation, he dealt with his grace not only for me but for others in and outside of the body of Christ. And the Lord dealt with me about forgiveness, and I had to forgive others. How can I freely accept his forgiveness yet deny others to be forgiven? He made me understand, yes, this person hurt you, but who have you hurt?

It would help if you walked through the healing from your hurt. It was my mirror image through his word, which showed me who I was, not the image I showed others. All these revelations helped me heal in so many areas of my life. I kept my focus on that thought during my transformation. The Lord is doing this because he loves me and doesn't want me to think I'm in the right relationship with him, and I'm not.

After the transformation of my heart, the Lord spoke to me a lot, and I could hear him so clearly now. Our relationship was getting stronger, and I could hear his instruction and follow them immediately. One day, as I was journaling, the Lord told me I was a divine dictator. He explained as he talked, and I would write down what he divinely said.

He later explained that I would minister to the heart of the drama. The plays would minister the message of the gospel and healing to the audience's hearts while attending each play. This was so true. After so many performances, people would come up to me and say, I got the message; that was for me. All the Lord wanted was to get his message of love, hope, and repentance to the people so the hearts of his children would return to him.

From that play, I've written and recorded songs. Some have a soundtrack for my first sold-out stage play. God uses me to help others know him as a healer through all the pain, healing, and hurt. So, wherever you are in your life, know that God's plan for your life is more significant than what you are going through.

In 2021, while journaling, the Lord told me that I was a writer and that I would write a book about having an intimate relationship with the Lord. I will share some of the Divine Intimate Conversations in the book. Each page is filled with love and passion for one another.

I can't describe love with words, yet I feel his passion and fire for me every morning as I sit in his presence. This is one of my Divine Intimate Conversations with the Lord! As I look into this New Year, I long for you, JESUS, to become the one thing that everything else in my life revolves around. The one thing that everything else in my life flows through. Today, looking to CHRIST gives me a goal to pursue, enjoy, and feel the passion. Because the most crucial relationship that matters for eternity is my relationship with YOU! JESUS CHRIST, TOGETHER FOREVER IN ETERNITY.

As I close my chapter, I pray that each woman reading my story will realize that our heavenly Father love's us so much. He gave His life for us. He has placed other women like me to share their stories from their hearts to save, empower, restore, and help my sisters to their divine place in the Lord. With all your strength, push past the pain, hurt, trauma, and heartache in your life. Remember, my story is coming from my heart. I extend my hand personally to you. Today, I am empowering you with words, but GOD positions your hearts for his healing purpose. God bless you.

Beverly LaRue

ABOUT THE AUTHOR

BEVERLY LARUE

Beverly LaRue has been a playwright since 2013. She has two children and three grandchildren. Over the years, she has written various plays addressing family unity, understanding the importance of a father, not judging others, building a relationship with God, sisterly love, bullying, etc. Her plays have a message mixed with love, laughter, and an eternal message. Beverly enjoys interacting with children of all ages in the community. Her plays were performed at Prairie State College and on other platforms in the community. She taught a playwriting 101 class at the Harvey Public Library for children ages 9-16. The students wrote their own scripts and performed the play on stage for the community. Beverly feels that there is no age limit when sharing drama.

She has instructed daycare and after-care children ages 7-12 for several weeks with her creative play sessions, incorporating drama into everyday play. Her love for the community is shown by donating tickets to various organizations that help people in need. Some of her Black History plays in 2019 and 2020 are: "Black History is everywhere (Part one) and Black History is everywhere, every day (Part two). Her plays were accessible to the public at the John D. Rita Recreation Center in Blue Island and Posen, Illinois, schools. Her passion for showcasing drama in various ways is shown through her gifted flexibility in promoting drama. Her play "My Hopeless Nosey Neighbor" was performed in an Orland Park senior living facility for senior residents. She turned the facility's dining room into an astonishing theater. The local newspaper shared her event with the community for an unforgettable evening shared with friends and families. The evening was breathing taking. Everyone marveled at the spectacular feeling of being at the theater. Beverly's cast performed two plays: The Father's Impact and Jr.'s Defense, one evening for a special Father's Day event that included dinner, with every father receiving a gift.

For Breast Cancer Month in 2019, Beverly wrote the play "The New Me I Didn't Want to Be. The play showed women with breast cancer facing challenges privately and in silence daily. Beverly was interviewed on TV about her creative playwriting skills for that performance.

Beverly has been interviewed several times on Gospel Radio. She is best known for "Sharing the heart of drama" on stage. She has written a book "'Divine Intimate Conversations,'" and it will be out soon. Her Inspirational Stage play "Sisters Plotting In The Pew" was performed at Mission Covenant Church in Blue Island in 2021. Look for her up-and-coming plays "Why Is She Hollering At Me?" and "It's Not About Your Body Baby! Beverly's greatest passion is sharing the love of God to others in a way that opens their hearts with the knowledge of knowing and loving Jesus Christ. She is the "Minister of Drama."

CHAPTER SEVEN

Real or Reel: Two Sides of Reality

BY DR. MARLENA SHERMAN – LINTON

You Can't Trust Your Reality: Who Told You That Story?
"Reality is the leading cause of stress among those in touch with it." -Lily Tomlin

I was born a Baby Boomer. I was raised by silent-generation southern grandparents and influenced by the Pepsi Generation (aka Gen X), an era where women were burning their bras and declaring independence. If I remember correctly, by my 16th birthday, in "reel" life, Erica Kane was on her 5th husband on the daytime soap opera, All My Children, and in real life, Elizabeth Taylor was on husband number six or seven.

The music of that time reflected the changing social norms of the decades, fueling the fight for civil rights for minorities, women, and the anti-war movement played out in cities across America. Michael Jackson's moved on from his ABCs and debuted his solo album "Off the Wall." Even with triple-digit summer weather, we questioned whether the water was safe after "Jaws" opened in theaters. We had individuals walking around practicing their dance moves for the first time while listening to music on their Walkmans.

While many were contributing to history and the changing world, I was curled up with a book and my vivid imagination inside of my Pacoima, California home. For as long as I can remember, my daily plan was to stay in school and get an excellent job so I could reap the American Dream as my reward. But what appeared to be a typical American teenager's perception of reality, which seemed very accurate as reflected in my daily tasks, was far from a perfect truth of the world. Knowing what I did not know in my teenage years is the difference between reminiscing and recalling memories from the past and living in past realities.

While coming-of-age experiences make each generation distinct, it influences our mindset and how we view and navigate the world around us. Typically, illusions of our childhood expectations follow these perceptual processes and firmly indoctrinated stories that help us realistically perceive the world around us and assist us not to be fooled by a particular situation so that we see something that does not exist is incorrect. Still, our imagination or "why not and "how come" become the real tales of our mothers, grandmothers, friends, and the world at large about our Daddy's reality.

Being a baby boomer raised by a silent generation grandfather, I learned early to be seen and not heard. There is some benefit to this mindset and some not-so-good effect on your emotions because when I had questions about my Daddy, I always thought I was not permitted to ask. The world and our loved ones around us give only a snapshot of the events and often have a one-sided approach to the pictures they paint and the stories they narrate. Too often, a story is blown out of proportion, or information is passed on erroneously, and we latch on to it and run with it. And if you're like me, you create your own narrative or reality in your head, a story that supports the feeling you hold in my heart. If permitted to ask my daddy questions, I would have asked to hear my Daddy's truth, his reality, because it is the only way to "*know the truth,* [his truth] the truth will set you free." John 8:32 (NIV). That is if you let it. Will you let it?

What's The Truth: Mine, His, and the Truth?

"The truth will set you free. But not until it is finished with you." -David Foster Wallace

93

While "daddy issues" have no defined clinical definition, those who have survived know the pain of the memories of absent or emotionally unavailable fathers are living memories of the past that we clanged so tightly to that we cannot move on with our present reality. So how does a lack or an estranged relationship with one's father in childhood impact adulthood? While not a clinical term or a recognized disorder, daddy issues are the realities that keep so many women managing the fear of abandonment, feelings of insecurity, an inability to trust men, low expectations of men, and low expectations of themselves. And when not addressed, these women find themselves staying in unhealthy relationships or leaping from relationship to relationship, catapulted by the fear of being without a man or staying attached in a toxic situation.

Truth be told, I have never been a daddy-less daughter, but that was the story I told myself. James Bates, my maternal grandfather, was a bigger-than-life father who ruled his home with strict silent generation love and support. Our twentieth-century home definitely modeled hard work, loyalty, and a do-as-I-say environment. The son of a Mississippi sharecropper's Daddy, or Papa as we would later call him, lovingly didn't play when it came to respect and being a man to set his own rules and imposed his boundaries, especially those he felt were right, just, and fair. Papa's truth was found in the forties, tired of being on the losing end of sharecropping, where the amount of debt increased, keeping his family poor while the landowners made off with all of the profits from his family's labor. Papa stood up and challenged the boss man. Of course, challenging the boss man is never met with a warm reception and especially wasn't the popular thing to do in rural 1940s Mississippi. The truth, Papa's exodus from Mississippi, hopping that westbound freight train in the heat of that steamy southern summer night where the temperature hovered above 90°F with 90% humidity, was Doctor Marlena in the making.

All the years of feeling restricted by Papa's rules and wishing my real Daddy was raising me would somehow make doing what I wanted more accessible. The truth is those past rules and restrictions all began to make sense, lying strapped to that cold Holy Cross hospital bed in Mission Hills, California. Staring the end of your life in the face provides an interesting introspective into your reality. It's almost funny how being near death can shock our stored memories and emotions into sharp focus.

Amazingly, [to my surprise], I always had everything I needed to be the woman who navigated a sea of confusion, chaos, tragedy, and triumph [these things are called life]. You see, what I learned from my "rediscovering your destiny" experience is that having two daddies was God's plan [*God's truth*] to provide the right daddy for me in the right season. From hearing my father's story, I learned that young James Sherman, at 22, was not the father I needed during my formative years. He was searching for the man he was to become. True he was married with children, and his destiny journey of who God intended him to be was in progress. The truth is, being a baby boomer raised by a silent generation grandfather, I learned early that being silent allowed me to access situations, places, and people others only dream about. I learned how to make a well-informed decision based on facts and not let my emotions rule the day. Not being able to always ask the questions I had about my life piqued my curiosity. Coupled with an academic need to be perfect, I began to read and research everything. I created a mindset of needing to know and finding a way to live life on my terms, and that manifested into stories in my mind that supported the feeling I held in my heart. Papa taught me to challenge or question when a situation did not feel right, push "the envelope" if a decision was unfair, and when my intuition provided an alert.

My truth, silence, rules, and restrictions appeared to be tools of oppression, but they were character builders clothed in love and shaped in discipline. The tools learned during my formative years have served me well in adulthood. I've used these mindset tools to challenge the status quo, further my education, enhance my career, and, most notably, live my purpose passionately. Of course, I've celebrated mountain top moments, but honestly, the peace came in the inevitable losses when

I allowed God to work in me and through me. Driving me to be like Hezekiah [Isaiah 38:2-3 (NIV)], who "turned his face to the wall [during his most painful moments] and prayed to the Lord, remember, Lord [reminding God of his promises], how I have walked before you faithfully and with wholehearted devotion and have done what is good in your eyes." Inner peace calms the soul and is a gateway to God, who handles all obstacles and intimidating threats.

What's The Back Story: Making Peace with the Past *"Peace I leave with you; my peace I give you. I do not give to you as the world gives. Do not let your hearts be troubled, and do not be afraid." ~John 14:27 (NIV)*

How do you summon the courage and wisdom to accept the past and move on with your emotions intact? How do you deal with forgiveness? Is it a difficult question to answer when your feelings run very hot or icy cold? If gone unaddressed, the hurt of unfulfilled daddy-daughter dreams will upset your psyche and derail your inner peace. For far too many years to count, my emotions were attached to my abandonment story, where I repeatedly asked myself what my life would have been like had my father raised me. Fortunately, as an adult, I was able to ask my Daddy my "why" questions. But early on in my life, I could not accept his truth about *his* truth. Is that you? Have you been allowed to hear his truth but dismiss it because it is not the script you wrote about "why" he failed you?

As I began to forge a relationship with my father, I realized I first needed to approach the situation with an open mind, open heart, and a forgiving spirit to connect with the spirit of the "daddy" I no longer only desired to know but needed to know. During this process, I learned to give myself a fighting chance to build a relationship with my father. I had to approach it with a forgiving heart as a way for me to release myself from the negative emotions that fueled my fear. I suppose you find yourself stuck on "why" you did not have the ideal daddy growing up. Forgiveness may be the antidote needed to loosen the grip of "not believing you were enough" firm hold.

Lying strapped to that hospital bed after spending time unconscious [80 days], I no longer cared about the past "whys"; I had to accept the reality that yesterday and all the yesterdays before it was gone! When I did not wake up into consciousness after my heart stopped on the operating table. I discovered focusing on why something did not happen will only have you miss out on the peace and beauty of the gift of life that comes with trusting all of your unrealized yesterdays to God – living and being in the present is a far better gift and way to thrive.

Look back into your past to consider what you're protecting yourself from.

- What perceived threat about your absent/estranged father has you running in the other direction?
- What ways of being have you adopted to avoid your fears and frustrations?
- What actions do you take to avoid those threats?
- How has this way of being impacted the quality of your life, relationships, health, and career?
- What has this pattern cost you in life?
- How is it holding you back?
- What is it preventing you from creating?

Forgive, Heal and Move On
Forgiveness is the key to peace of the future and moving beyond difficult times.

I hope you become free emotionally to engage in the present gift. When you are genuinely emotionally free, you are free to build a better life and future for yourself and your loved ones. If you have endured a complicated past, use it as a learning resource, but don't live in it. Don't give your energy and power to someone who negatively influences any aspect of your life; instead, establish healthy boundaries with the people around you — and assume responsibility for your emotions and the stories you choose to believe.

Instead, cast your cares to God and trust your Heavenly Father and the forgiveness he grants all His children, even you. Refuse to occupy your mind with negative thoughts and feelings. Don't spend your time complaining or clinging to bad memories and longed-for interactions. If you don't know how to trust God, the Bible gives us much instruction when it comes to forgiveness. Here are a few verses that you can use to bridge the delta between the past and present to bring peace to your mind and build your strength.

- We forgive because God has forgiven us (Ephesians 4:32).
- We forgive in obedience to God (Matthew 6:14-15; Romans 12:18).
- We forgive others for gaining control of our lives from hurt emotions (Genesis 4:1-8).
- We forgive so we won't become bitter and defile those around us (Hebrews 12:14-15).

If I were a cat, my curiosity would have gotten me killed.
"Being inquisitive about other people's affairs may get you into trouble."
~Proverb

Stay mindful that no single answer will address your particular daddy's questions of why your Daddy's script of an estranged happy ever after, but forgiveness is a great starting place. You see, forgiveness is for you to regain control of your emotions; it can reconcile and restore your inner peace.

I remember that first Christmas and Daddy James was permitted to come to Papa's house. It was Christmas 1976, and my mother and father had come for Christmas dinner. I was standing in Mama Gina's kitchen, hearing her speak proudly about my report card, where I had scored several As and Bs. I listened to my Daddy James say, "Gina, that's nice, but what about this C in math." Before I knew what happened, I responded, "it wasn't like you were here to teach me."

Mama Gina, being the loving angel, apologized profusely and promptly told me to do the same. Quick to have a comeback, "No," I responded, and before that backhand slap appeared to my amazement and curiosity, my Daddy said, "that's okay, Gina, she's just like me," as he wrapped me in a bear hug. What does he mean just like him? He doesn't know me! How can I be like this stranger?

Curiosity would have me pushing up daisies if I were a cat because I wanted to know what he meant by "just like him." That day started a rain of emotions I didn't want to acknowledge. But the more I tried not to like my Daddy, the more I wanted to get to know him. I tried to understand what made him choose how he lived his life and what made my mother so crazy in love [using my Beyonce voice] with him that she would throw caution to the wind in the name of love. At times I was angry with myself for wanting to find out more about him when he was the cause of so much pain in my life.

When you have more questions than answers, your emotions can get the best of you. The drop-off-the-cliff rollercoaster of your emotions roadblocks the good intentions to move beyond a troubled heart. The most significant way to block the view of the present and future destinations is driving your car while only looking in the rearview mirror. Release the fear because trust and believe me, no amount of anger or unforgiveness can rewrite the past, and oh yeah, the curious cat only got wiser and freer.

Strangers
We're Just Strangers with Some Memories. ~ Unknown

Let me ask you a question. Would you be mad at the neighbor down on 112th Street if you never met him? No, right – how can you be mad at someone you never met? For years I walked around wearing my daddy issues around my neck like a badge of sadness, weighed down by the shame of not having my father love me enough to be my Daddy. But what if I told it was all self-induced from a reality I created? I'll repeat it if you missed my statement; I walked around mad at a total stranger because I did not know who my father was or what caused him to make the choices he made about his life or my life. But I held my brokenness against him because he didn't meet the expectations created in my mind and heart of the daddy role. Crazy, right? Even though I interacted with and saw my daddy often, I walked around mad at the stranger he was because he didn't fit the reality of who he was supposed to be in my life.

Where did I get these images of my daddy? Was it television? Or perhaps it was watching my friends with their fathers. Maybe it is wired into my unconscious mind, which is not too far off from reality because studies show that our hormones produce stress responses when we are around strangers. These stress responses create a rise in our cortisol, making us less empathetic as an unusual consequence. So, when we view our fathers as strangers because we do not know them well, we automatically think of them as someone who has done something to make us feel uncomfortable or someone who has the power to harm us, hurt us or take us away from what is familiar and safe. So, we shy away from getting to know them on a personal level and create a story as a way to conceal our inability to process our emotions. During childhood, I hid my fear of abandonment from my family and friends. I hid behind a mask of being okay! When I was not close to that in my feelings.

My mistrust impaired my ability to trust others and avoid any control or authority throughout my life. It was tough to get close to others or feel worthy or intimate around everyone, which led to fears of abandonment, anxiety, depression, codependence, or other issues. For years, I imagined that my future would magically repair what happened in my childhood once I got into a stable relationship. When that did not manifest, I hopped out of that relationship, at no fault of his, believing that I would find a way to avoid the pain as quickly and swiftly as possible. Instead of resolving my issues, I would focus on "past pain" and move on to the following situation without reconciling my feelings.

Not addressing my issues created somewhat of a "lily pad hopping" experience. Before one lily pad would sink, I would hope for the next relationship and leave the last relationship floundering and sinking on its own. I wanted nothing to do with keeping the relationship afloat as I felt it wasn't my responsibility, and I certainly did not want to go down with the ship, to say. I would do this with relationships, jobs, friends, family, projects, and goals to avoid leaving; I would go emotionally. It wasn't until I coded on the operating table and spent 80 days in a coma that I realized I could no longer search for the answer to the question [why aren't I enough?] that kept me stuck, looking outside for an answer. Laying there, I thought over the stories that got me to that point. If I had the function of my hand, you would have found me scratching my head, wondering, "How did I get here?" You would have seen fear in my eyes, not knowing where I was going. Would I die and pass to my four sons' abandonment issues?

I was struck with the reality that I had been wearing a false mask for the entirety of my life. The realities painted and dictated by my environment have fostered a need to blame my daddy for my life not being the picture-perfect life. The answers I needed were stored on the inside, locked in my unconscious mind, and the only way to manage my daddy issues was to deal with my feeling and emotions by opening my mind, heart, and feeling to find and experience the peace that my soul desired.

As scary as it was to face my fears of abandonment, lying strapped to that hospital bed with nowhere to go and no one to talk to but God. Coming face to face with death, personal imperfections, and the inability to see that every person has a story of their truth put my life into perspective. A reality that made me get creative with forgiveness quickly because the weapon formed against me was my heart's inability to forgive. Reflecting on that dark period of my near-death struggle, I lost everything important to me because of false evidence appearing real in a blinking of an eye. I was able to release it all to the Lord, the only one who had stayed with me the entire journey of my life. "Fear not, for I am with you; be not dismayed, for I am your God; I will strengthen you, I will help you, I will uphold you with my righteous right hand. Behold, all who are incensed against you shall be put to shame and confounded; those who strive against you shall be as nothing and shall perish. You shall seek those who contend with you, but you shall not find them; those who war against you shall be as nothing at all. For I, the Lord your God, hold your right hand; it is I who say to you, "Fear not, I am the one who helps you.' Isaiah 41:10-13 (ESV). And like for me, the Creator has a great plan for you, and He intends to use you in wonderful and unexpected ways if you allow Him, but first, you must make peace with your father of the past.

Choice This Day

"Choose this day whom you will serve." Joshua 24:15 (KJV)

Failing to focus on the dreams and visions of prosperity, we fill our minds with "what ifs," "how comes," and "whys." Being imperfect as a person whose emotions run wild will keep your thoughts out of control, making you feel stuck in the claws of the past even when your mind knows different. Because of our unaddressed emotions, we cannot let the pain go associated and will again suffer the predictability of the universal consequences.

Fifteen years later, I found myself looking down the barrel of the past with an opposite mindset. A mindset embraces what the Bible instructs us to do in Philippians 3:23-14 (NKJV). "I do not count myself to have apprehended, but one thing *I do,* forgetting those things which are behind and reaching forward to those things which are ahead, I press toward the goal for the prize of the upward call of God in Christ Jesus." While not simple or easy, begin to celebrate this day with praise on your lips and hope in your heart. When focusing on the promises of what is for you versus focusing on what happened to you, we can begin navigating the future from a more optimistic perspective. Focusing on the past is futile; the past never moved the needle onto a place of happiness or contentment. The wise learned that no matter the bitterness or anger you hold onto, it can't change or won't change what happened yesterday. Forgiving yourself and continuing to forgive yourself is the only thing that genuinely freed me from past regrets, worries, and complaints of an unfulfilled reality. Learning to control your negative emotions and clear the past by planning for the process will take time, patience, and practice. The beauty of God's Holy Word will provide guidance if you are genuinely willing to search for the wisdom needed to live in peace. Then and only then can the heart live with confidence and courage when the mind allows it to achieve the goal of accepting your reality was made just for you and nobody else.

Wisdom is the principal thing;Therefore get wisdom.
And in all your getting, get understanding.
~Proverbs 4:7 (NKJV)

Here's a little self-reflection work for you. Absentee/estranged father:

1. Are you upset with him?
2. Are you trying to forgive him for the guilt you carry?
3. Was there anyone who filled that father role?
4. If you have had multiple father figures, which one do you honor?
5. Make a list of the daddy issues that darken your heart's ability to shine. Then, pray about your list and turn it over to God.

"If you are God's child, you are no longer bound to your past or to what you were.
You are a brand-new creature in Christ Jesus." ~ Kay Arthur

"This means that anyone who belongs to Christ has become a new person. The old life is gone; a new life has begun!" ~ 2_Corinthians 5:17 (NLT)

Dr. Marlena Sherman-Linton

ABOUT THE AUTHOR

DR. MARLENA SHERMAN-LINTON

Dr. Marlena Sherman Linton is the published author of Rediscovering Your Destiny: The Power of Possibilities and How to Reinvent the Inevitable and is the Founder of MSL Global Development, LLC. In addition, she is the creator of the Purpose & Passion Transformational Lifestyle program.

She holds a Ph.D. from Colorado Technical University in Management with a concentration in Organizational Development & Change. Along with being a Mindset Development Expert, Dr. Marlena empowers individuals with the strategies to rediscover their lost identities, redefine their lives, and reinvent their self-confidence. Her coaching allows her clients to become more self-aware of their ability to connect with other people personally and professionally.

Promoting Purpose and Passion in every step of her journey, Dr. Marlena, a Sepsis infection survivor, knows what it takes to fight back from the dead, literally! Having spent eleven weeks on life support and being hospitalized for six months, she is a real "walking miracle." Learning to walk, talk, and write all over again, she set out to understand her purpose for surviving such a near-death medical complication when most do not.

Feeling the need to do more, Dr. Marlena is now committed to empowering individuals searching for their identity and self-worth to live out their purpose and passion. Dr. Marlena is a sought-after conference speaker, inspirational motivator, consultant, trainer, and #1 Amazon Best Selling Author.

With over 30 years of HR experience, she (most recently) served as the Corporate Director of Human Resources at a high-profile aviation solution company. Dr. Marlena is also internationally known as an accomplished mentor and advisor. She understands what is needed to touch hearts and change minds for the better. Dr. Marlena knows how to cut the chains of negative emotions that keep so many anchored to the past.

Dr. Marlena holds many other degrees and certificates from some of the most prestigious universities and organizations. Always a student and, more than ever, the teacher. She loves to travel and spend time with family and friends.

You can find Dr. Marlena at https://www.DrMarlena360.com

CHAPTER EIGHT

Second Coming Rebirth the Set-Up.... In the Beginning

BY ROCHELLE ANDERSON - MOORE

As I started writing my manuscript titled; Second Coming Rebirth, I allowed fear to step in. Fear of what my family would say and if they would understand. What encouraged me to write? My purpose for writing is to empower others who have experienced sexual abuse, incest, or molestation. What inspired me to write the Second Coming Rebirth manuscript many years after my childhood? I had a story to tell. I lived my life helping and protecting others who experienced the same violations in their lives and struggled to release the hurt, mistrust, and pain.

My parents migrated from Mississippi to the North to East St. Louis, Illinois, for better working and living conditions. I am the youngest of my mother's and father's children. We were all born at Barnes Maternity as they were the only hospital that would deliver Black children at that time.

What do you do when you are unaware that your world was shattered, never to be the same again? Before age five, your body was violated and treated as an adult body. I was aware of the feelings but not understanding my emotions. Unfortunately, I know I am not alone. Numerous women and men have had their bodies and minds tampered with, misused, and abused during the early stages of their lives.

The journey from an abusive childhood to becoming a teenager through adulthood is challenging. The sexual abuse with my father ended when my menstrual cycle started. However, it was just the beginning. Please bear with me as I share more pain and sorrow at the hands of the man I thought loved me, my father.

When I was three years old, the youngest of my siblings, my father was a cab driver and worked on the railroad. He sought employment at American Motors in Wisconsin for better job opportunities to support our family. Due to my mother working and my siblings being in school, as the youngest, I traveled with my father for five years back and forth on weekends. In addition, my family would come to visit us in Wisconsin on holidays.

I stayed with my Aunt and Uncle and their children while my father worked. We would go back and forth to Wisconsin several times a month. There were also times when I would stay with my relatives, who were more like my sisters and brothers. As I traveled with my father, as a three-year-old, I would stand next to him in the front seat while he drove.

As a child, I was unaware of what was taking place. Other males were touching my body inappropriately. I didn't know how to say stop. Eventually, when I turned five, we all moved to our new home in Wisconsin. The abuse from my father did not stop but continued until my menstrual cycle began. We lived on a busy street, and as I played in the front yard, men would blow their horns (at me) and occasionally pull over, saying things about my body and asking me to come to their cars. This scared me and confused me as a young child. I did not understand it all.

I started spending the night at one of my girlfriend's houses. Not only did her brothers molest me, but her father also molested me. It was at their house that I started my menstrual cycle years later. Her mother called my mother. No one told me about having a menstrual cycle. In my mind, it was my friend's mother who taught me. I thought God was punishing me for allowing these things to happen to me. I never told my mother. She was already going through so much; I didn't want to put anything else on her plate. I stayed silent.

As I continued to mature, I started wearing what I called a Bohemian style of clothing to hide my curves. However, I was scared and confused at a young age and did not understand why I received all this attention. In addition, men on the Deacon Board at church would say inappropriate comments.

Both of my brothers went into the military. One was drafted, and the other enlisted voluntarily.

I believe now that it was to get away from the abuse that was taking place. I now realize how difficult it was for all of us. One day, I woke up, and my parents were arguing. My mother found some savings bonds with a child's name on them. I later found it to be my brother from another mother. So I eventually ended up with three siblings under me with three different mothers. Oops, four! I'll get to that later.

My oldest brother was like a father to me. My brother returned home from the military with his beautiful wife from Jamaica. I remember he would drive me to school and have me read the billboards. My brother noticed I struggled to see the billboard. He shared this with my mother, and she had my eyes examined. After that, he became a teacher and basketball coach, and everybody loved him.

As I matured, I believed that sex was Love or sex meant that person loved me. It sometimes felt good because I didn't feel any real love or healthy fatherly attention, nor did I live seeing my father showing my mother any real passion or healthy attention.

I stayed involved in school, choir, track and field, church, and the drum and bugle corps. I wanted to stay away from home. One day I called myself running away from home.

I became promiscuous and related the sexual activities (that I engaged in) to Love. I recall a Saturday night I went to a club with a girlfriend. I had been drinking, and alcohol became my outlet. I left my girlfriend and got a ride home with this guy. He took me to a motel; as we walked into the room, numerous guns were lying on the bed.

Of course, my "high" went away immediately, and I was frightened and started crying. I had no escape and continued allowing this guy to abuse me. Once again, I could not use my voice. When I arrived home, my mother made me sit at the table. I smelled of alcohol, and my makeup was smeared on my face. She made me eat breakfast and would not allow me to change clothes. I attended church and sat in the front row with her in front of the Pastor. I was so embarrassed! My mother used this opportunity to teach me a lesson.

MY JOURNEY THRU SILENT TEARS....

At nineteen years old, I married a physically abusive man. He didn't work, and he would drive me to work daily. I would give him money for cigarettes and drinks. One night he didn't come to pick me up. I needed a ride, so a male friend took me home. When I arrived home, he was not there but arrived later. He was intoxicated while asking me how I got home. He stated that I was supposed to wait for him. I told him a friend had given me a ride home.

We lived in his parent's basement. He started beating me in my stomach and asked me why I wasn't getting pregnant. I ran upstairs but tripped on my gown during the process. He caught me, grabbed my face, and hit it against the wooden steps numerous times. Finally, I got away from him because I ran upstairs, only to have his mother grab me. I told her to let me go! I wanted to see my face. Initially, she wouldn't, but she finally did. I SCREAMED IN HORROR when I looked at my face because my cheekbone protruded beyond its normal shape.

That was the day I left him, but he wasn't through with me. So I skipped work and found an apartment. One day as I was hanging up pictures on the wall, I heard noises on my balcony. Now mind you, I lived on the second floor. Someone suggested I never move into a first-floor bottom apartment as a single person. So I was afraid not to let him in, as he was banging on the glass.

He entered my apartment and began telling me that he was taking me to work, and he will pick me up, and I better be there whenever he got there. As he entered the room, I looked at the hammer. My initial thought was to pick up the hammer and hit him to protect myself. My next thought was, what if he takes the hammer from me and kills me?

My words to myself were, "I could beat him to a pulp where no one would recognize him" however, my next thought was that if he took the hammer from me and beat me, I wouldn't be recognizable. So, I left the hammer alone while he pushed me down the stairs to take me to work. The street getting to my employment was busy all the time. On that day, he drove 80 miles an hour. He did not stop for any lights or cars. When we arrived at my job, and I was getting out of the car, he said, kiss me, and you better be here when I come to pick you up. So, I kissed him, saying, this is the last time. This time I used my voice. I was proud of myself as I walked away.

While working my shift, my co-workers saw bruises on my arms ever since I started working there. They were always giving me support and asking me what they could do. I didn't ever think I would find myself in the same situation as my mother. I never told my parents until I left. I had my father come and get me and my belongings. I knew my father always carried a gun. This one time, my father made me feel safe.

Reflecting on past years, I realize that God used my pain as my purpose to allow me to help others. In my past and today in the present, others sought me out on different issues. However, God had to heal me first, and I eventually learned to forgive my father.

NO FATHERS LOVE

Back in the day, my father owned and worked in his Bar during the day. When I went to his Bar, he would act like a great, incredible father. I would use those times to ask him for money. Outside of the Bar, he would typically say no. However, while working at the Bar, he liked to be seen as this loving father.

In my city, they offer discounted movie tickets on Saturdays. My friends and I would go to the movies every Saturday. I had a great time hanging out with my friends. One Saturday, my friends and I were going into the theater while my father was coming out with this woman and a young child. Later, I found out it was him (the little boy with the strange lady) and his mother whom they were arguing about. As my friends stated, I was embarrassed: who is that little boy and lady with your Dad? As a family, I don't believe we ever healed the trauma we faced at a young age.

My eyes filled with sadness, and my soul felt sorrow from never becoming my Dad's prize. That little child inside me missed how a man should have treated his wife, his Queen, and the Mother of his children. That child was never taught self-worth, from never hearing the words I love you, and I will protect you.

These eyes have cried silent tears of pain, hurt, shame, unworthiness, and the feeling of not being enough. My mind experienced fear, the inability to trust, and, more importantly, the inability to be myself. My eyes sought joy, and my soul sought Love and peace.

I did not feel Love and peace for or from my father during this period. I felt used.

When I reflect on years past, I realize that God used my pain for his purpose to allow me to help others. However, God had to heal me first. During my healing, I eventually learned how to forgive my father.

MY JOURNEY THRU SILENT TEARS

I wasted (in some ways) so many years of my life. I used drugs, sex, and downright procrastination, but mostly fear. I've learned to forgive. I released those I thought to be my soul mates. These men misused my body and took my innocence. Also, I freely gave my body away.

As I rewind, I visualize standing in front of others in a program that I called 'Living Free' with confidence, strength, wisdom, and grace. Thank you, Lord, for continuing to guide my footsteps. I asked God to remove distraction, procrastination, fear, and laziness from my negative habits so I could walk in abundant grace and mercy. I have been hurt before, but my capacity for Love is far greater than my pain!!

Questions to answer for yourself, about yourself:

1. What have you told yourself you couldn't do because of a childhood story?
2. How has this affected your relationships?
3. What benefits did you get from that childhood story?
4. How would your mother, father, or siblings describe you?
5. What personal conversations do you reveal to a stranger on a plane?
6. What do you tell about yourself to new people you meet when networking?
7. What do you share about your life, past, and childhood with friends you haven't seen in 20 years? In other words, do you tell them all the dirt?
8. What don't you reveal to anyone in the previous question?

RESIST FEAR…. REGAIN FAITH AND RECEIVE FAVOR

I had to expect and believe in the worthiness I have been embracing through the Love of God.

My mother developed and was diagnosed with breast cancer after hitting her breast on the tub twice within a short period. During that time, I worked for AT&T. As a family, we set up a schedule so we could help take care of her. I did not have a vehicle and lived within walking distance of my job. As we were making schedules for her care, my employer worked with me to help create an acceptable plan.

My mother gave me her car to get to my sister's house, thirty minutes from my job in a different city. We made it work with my sister, her husband, and my aunt. Unfortunately, my mother passed away when I was twenty-four years old. Before her passing, as she lay in the hospital, she shared (with me) that although I was the youngest, I was the strongest and wisest. I was unsure how to take her words but realized she knew what I had been going through with my father. I was too young to lose my mother. The days that followed were a blare.

My grandmother was also in the hospital, not knowing her daughter was in the next room dying. Immediately after my mother passed, my father told me to bring him her car. I told him she gave me her car to come back and forth to see her and assist in her care. She wanted me to have it.

After my grandmother's funeral service, my father had the car towed the next day. I was so devastated, and I called him and cussed him out. He was every MotherFxxxr in the book. My exact words to him were: "Until I can talk to you like you are my father; you are just another nigger in the street."

When my neighborhood friends walked home, this little girl waited on the steps to greet her cousins returning from school. My friends would also tell me that she looked like me. I would always say no-she does not. One day as I passed her, we looked at each other, and my thoughts were, she does look like me. I thought to myself; maybe she was my sister.

After my mother's death, my father took my siblings to Chicago to his sister's house to discuss his desire to remarry. I was not asked how I felt about it. My eldest brother had returned home from the military and was married to a beautiful Jamaican woman he met in Panama. They had two beautiful children. My brother became a teacher and basketball coach. He also worked at the Bar with my father.

The night of my brother's death was very traumatic. I received a call telling me to come to the hospital immediately. I arrived and wanted to see him badly. However, the doctors would not allow me to see my brother. It was hard for me. I kept screaming, "I needed to see him." My spirit was also saying the same thing. But unfortunately, it was not possible because he was shot in the head. Not seeing him until the funeral was devastating to me.

As I stated earlier, my mother died in June of 1980. My grandmother and brother died in April of 1981, and my Grandfather died in September 1981. I was devastated by all these deaths in a short period. Sadly, my child would never physically know my mother or brother, but only through my stories.

FEAR FAITH AND FAVOR

I asked God to remove the fear of being a faithful wife, being a mother as I was with child, and moving to another state away from family. My husband had an opportunity to relocate to Ohio. I was able to transfer my AT&T position. Many people who transferred to Ohio used drugs during that period. I found myself away from my family, raising a child.

I worked for AT&T. I took advantage of an opportunity to attend the University of Toledo. Unfortunately, achieving my bachelor's degree in Social Work took me years. However, I can be honest and say that the demons of sexual abuse, unfaithfulness in my marriage, and drug usage continued to plague me.

SECOND COMING REBIRTH

I will never forget the day I received a call from my father's wife as I was preparing to shower. She shared with me that the police had just served my father with papers regarding the sexual abuse of a minor. She wanted me to come over and help her understand this unwanted revelation.

I was an APSW - Advanced Practice Licensed Social Worker, working with Children and Families regarding child welfare and juvenile behaviors and children in Foster Care.

I cried, asking God, why me? I didn't like her (my father's wife), and we never talked. She would call my sisters and brother, but I didn't care. Then, she disrespected my mother by having an affair and having a child with my father. Then, to add another insult, my father moved her into the house, the same place my parents worked to obtain for us.

We had one room in our den, and we called it our Shrine. There were only pictures of me, my siblings, and our children. Not her child or grandchildren. Their photos were in other places throughout the house.

As I showered, my tears would not stop. As I write this section, my emotions rise, and tears fall from my eyes. Thoughts and feelings of losing my Mother, my Brother, Father resurfaced as my whole life flashed before me. India Arie's song, 'I am Light,' started playing. I prayed to God to give me the strength to have this conversation with my father's wife.

As I got out of the shower, I ran my hand over my face, removing myself. Then, I put on my professional face. I got dressed and went to my father's house. When I got there, I looked at the papers. I told my 70-something-year-old father and his wife that he was facing 20 years in prison for the sexual abuse of a minor. I also told them a child was conceived. Then, I suggested they call a family meeting, as we all had children in the school district.

My father's wife wanted his children (me included) to go with them to see his Attorney and say what a good father he was. I knew if I went, I could not honestly say he was a good father. So, I used my position as a Social Worker, working daily with sexually abused children by adults, as my reason for not attending.

My father became speechless and ended up with trauma-based Dementia. So, I decided to start going to his house on Sundays after church. I didn't want to have any regrets. On some Sundays, I could only stay for a short time, like fifteen minutes. Other times I would stay for dinner. Visiting my father was my way of letting him know I forgave him a long time ago.

I had to forgive my father in order for me to continue doing the work I was doing to heal myself. I would use my lunch breaks to see my therapist at one point. When I first went, I cried the whole time. After a few sessions, she recommended that I take medication to avoid crying throughout the session. I finally agreed. I wanted to share this with my siblings, but I learned to be silent.

My sister is the First Lady of her Church. She started having yearly Women's Retreats. For years I would attend. While attending the women's retreat, layers of my abusive life peeled away each year. I would leave with more confidence, thanking God for my Blessings of helping others heal.

After the last retreat, I was at work when my sister called. She wanted me to meet her at my older sister's house, as she was very emotional and needed us to come over. I got there first, and soon as she opened the door, she apologized for not believing me all these years. Then, when my other sister got there, we affectionately embraced each other. That was one of the greatest gifts God could have given me after having to hold this secret all my life. That moment is still worth more than money can buy.

Sometimes I would wonder what my life would have been like if I did not have those experiences. Yet, I know my desire to help others was (and still is) real. Helping others is more important than helping myself.

I was confident not to let people know my story, hurts, and pains. What's that song; You don't know my story, all the things that I've been through, you can't feel my pain, all the things I did to get here.

I would always ask God this question: What is my purpose? I knew it couldn't be to continue on the path I was on. I knew God had a plan for me. I always believed that all things happen for a reason. If my experiences in life had not happened, I don't know what I could have become. Those experiences gave me the tools to continue my Souls' Journey of helping others. I felt it was time to share my story and experiences in hopes of helping other women who are suffering in silence and need healing, caring, and understanding.

119

I AM LIGHT. I am the transformational change that was needed for me to push forward. If I can thrive and not just survive, so can you. As I reach out across the time and space that separates us, may my story touch your heart, mind, body, spirit, and soul. Change is not change - until change occurs. When you change the way you look at yourself, the self you look at will change! Yes, I am a changed, empowering woman.

Rochelle Anderson – Moore

ABOUT THE AUTHOR

ROCHELLE ANDERSON – MOORE

During her tenure, Rochelle had a deep passion and a long-serving history of working with communities in need. She was an Advanced Practice Social Worker and a Licensed Clinical Social Worker for the Kenosha County Division of Children and Family Services in Wisconsin. Rochelle strived to inspire hope, activate purpose, create change, and help others find empowerment while providing solution-focused mental health services. Rochelle independently conducted mental health assessments and provided wellness checks and ongoing monitoring of patients with psychiatric needs.

In 1997, she received her Bachelor of Arts Degree in Social Work from the University of Toledo. In 2003, she received her Master of Social Work from Loyola University, Chicago, at Carthage College/Kenosha Wisconsin Campus. In 2005, she was the Race, Culture, and Ethnicity Curriculum Instructor at Loyola University, Carthage College/Kenosha Campus.

In 2007, Rochelle performed her civic duty as an Adjunct Social Worker Instructor teaching Family Violence at Loyola University Chicago/ Kenosha Campus.

January 2014 - 2016: Rochelle became a Clinical Case Manager with Community Care Resources Inc. Rochelle provided ongoing support to children and families in Foster homes while educating and teaching parents, families, and staff on prevention and treatment intervention techniques. She independently conducted psychological, alcohol, and other drug assessments and identified DSM-5 mental health diagnoses. She was trained and qualified in TAT -Trauma Assessment Tool practical implantation.

January 2004 - Present: Rochelle works with Moore and Associates Living Free -AODA Program. She teaches and facilitates Anger Management and Criminal Thinking curriculums to incarcerated females in a 12 - week program to discourage and eliminate alcohol and drug usage and abuse. She also educates and encourages females to obtain life and social skills to become productive contributors to their communities. Rochelle is available for book signings, speaking engagements, panel discussions, and conversations about how to best help and serve others.

Rochelle Anderson – Moore
Email: sisterangel31@yahoo.com

CHAPTER NINE

Evolution of A Butterfly

BY MAQUIRA OLIVER

Emergence: The process of coming into view or becoming exposed after being concealed.

I was raised in a large extended family, as my mother has seven sisters and one brother. I have twenty-five cousins, and we are all around the same age. We were raised together like brothers and sisters. However, there are only five girl cousins within our generation, which made us spend a lot of time together. We were all taught by my grandmother that family was most important. We were to trust family over friends because our family was all we had!

In retrospect to my mother's large family, my father's side consisted of three siblings, two brothers, and one sister. I have nine cousins, a balance of five girls and four boys. Our grandparents kept us together, specifically my grandmother. She was serious about reading, education, and teaching us survival skills like cooking, sewing, and gardening. My father's mother cherished all her grandchildren as we were her everything.

My parents conceived me while my father was still in college. He attended Morehouse in Atlanta, and my mother stayed in Michigan. However, I don't remember when he wasn't present; she and my father's people were instrumental in raising my two younger brothers and me. We had a typical sister, brother relationship.

I spent a lot of time at one of my aunt's homes with my cousin, who is like my best friend and sister. We did everything together, played with dolls, did each other's hair, read, and cleaned. We would stay up all night telling each other our secrets and dreams. I remember spending a lot of time together on weekends and through the summer. We were two peas in a pot. The lady next door would braid our hair and put beads on them. Our mothers always dressed us up. The dresses had the bells sewn into the hems at the bottom of the dresses, along with matching socks that had big lace wrapped around our ankles. Things back then seemed normal, and life was good.

My memories go back to when I was about eight years old. A group of boys around my age was upstairs in the bedroom, watching television and hanging out, including myself. It started as a game on a sunny day, but I've lost some details. I remember the bed being pushed against the back wall. Next, one of the boys asked me to lie on my tummy. Another boy used a sandwich bag before he encouraged me to lie there. I remember him teasing me for not properly cleaning myself, and he told me I was dirty. Later, another boy led me to the main bathroom, and I remember the pink tile midpoint up the walls as he sat on the toilet. Next, he made me kneel on the floor and instructed me to put my mouth on him and think of his penis like candy. I remember the sandwich bag covering the shaft of his penis. I can remember an older woman talking with us later that day, and I think she also called the police, but that memory is vague. I remember us sitting in the living room and talking, and it felt serious.

By the time I was twelve years old. I learned that men saw something I didn't quite understand in me. I stayed with my aunt that summer, mainly to spend time with my best friend. Her brothers had friends across the street that would come to visit. One of their friends came over one day, and he spent a lot of time with my aunts because he was visiting his family for the summer. I can remember him being tall and slender with a dark completion. We were upstairs in the attic watching television on this day. It was just him and I, and we were small talking when he asked me if I knew how to kiss or if I had kissed a boy before. I think I told him, "No." I remember him forcing his tongue into my mouth, and his hands were all over me. I remember feeling angry and overwhelmed. I remember him fighting me, and his tongue felt nasty and horrible. His hands were locked tight, but I managed to rip away from him.

From that point forward, I felt like a walking sex magnet. Men would yell at me out the windows of their cars when I would ride my bike or walk down the street. Those who I thought were friends would try to force me to have sex with them. I was stronger by then and able to fight them off because I was just as strong and sometimes stronger than my attackers.

I never spoke of what happened to me, not even to my parents or closest friends. Family stuck together. I thought the rest was normal. It just didn't always feel good.

I met my first boyfriend when I was age thirteen. We met at a skating rink, and he was extra sweet to me. We would regularly visit each other, and he would buy me things, take me to the movies, and I would go to church with his family. He was my first at everything nice - My first date, my first boyfriend, my first piece of jewelry. I gave myself to him by the time I was fifteen years old, and we stayed together until I was in the $10^{th}/11^{th}$ grade, until he moved away. Then, when I was a freshman in college, we rekindled our relationship, and I became pregnant with our first child. I was terrified to tell my parents. I knew they would be disappointed and angry with me. And I wanted to keep my child. It took me about a month to tell them, and when I did, my mother was disappointed but supportive.

On the other hand, my father wrote me a heartfelt letter to share his dismay about my pregnancy. He noted that I would not amount to much of anything! My friends would be better than me, and he would not help me from this point forward. I never felt such shame. This became my turning point as I decided to do it all independently. At least, I thought I could. I stayed with my parents long enough to birth my son and get back to school. My mother helped me get a car with the funds my grandmother left after her passing.

After taking the winter semester of 1999 off, I went to a community college that spring and summer, then returned to my university in the fall of '99. My son and I would stay with my grandmother, and we traveled to school from her home. I could remember when my close friend would let us stay with him. He would sneak us into his dorm because children were prohibited from staying overnight. He was my only close platonic male friend at that time, a true friend. He would keep my son while I was in class and encouraged me to stay in school. Then, my God-sister, let us move with her for a little while. She would also help me watch my son while I was in school, working, or doing a little dating.

Over the next twenty years, I began spiraling down several unhealthy relationships, including the most important one, the one with myself. I have experienced physical abuse, including black eyes, endless nights of fights, car windows busted out, and hurtful name-calling, all with my 2-year-old son watching. I can recount men laying guns on my chest to intimidate me. Men would say that my mouth was too slick, or I wasn't shit but a bitch that thought she was too good. By the time my son reached age twenty, I had experienced men breaking into my home, stalking me on more than one occasion, and more than two attempts of being sexually assaulted. I experienced manipulation and countless acts of physical abuse beyond black eyes. I recall having lumps on the right side of my head underneath my hair with extreme headaches. I have walked through the front door of my home, where I raise my children, to find the back windows busted out and water pouring from every faucet. He even pulled the water hose into my bedroom to flood my mattress. If that wasn't a message blaring in my face, I don't know what was! It took me three years to fully recover and feel comfortable in my home.

By this time, I had acquired my master's degree in Social Work and was working towards gaining my full license to practice as a Clinical Social Worker for the State of Michigan. I have been providing therapy to many women and men. I often had conflicts with hearing stories from those who came to me for internal healing—many of them praising the work I provided for them. However, I would sit in frustration and anger while reflecting on my life. I became full of grief, anger, and resentment. Can you understand where I'm coming from by sharing these feelings?

My grief came from how my life "should have been." My father's words rang in my ears, constantly reminding me that I was a failure. I would watch my friends move along with their lives as they progress in their careers and families. I would question why I was without someone to pull me by my ear, sit me down, and have that "Chil, what are you doing and why?" talk. I thought everyone had that special someone they could depend on to rescue them. Where was my person!?!

I felt judged, angry, and alone! No matter how hard I tried, I could not escape the drama that plagued my life. Although I kept constantly running into men that fixated and perpetrated on the existence of my ass, I began to take refuge in that role. I thought I could be more intelligent (than that) and use my superpower, but it (sex) ate me alive. With every punch in my face or penetration into my body, toxicity grew along with the poisonous experiences that left me unaware. I was toxic in every aspect of my life except for my job. Everyone saw it but me.

I was fighting recklessness. I would freely give of myself because I wanted someone to value and desire me for more than my pussy, or is it my ass!!! I felt like my total body was becoming numb, and I soon began to reject any man who attempted to get close to my emotional being. Men made me angry, especially my father, because I felt I could not depend on him. His words (me being a failure) would drive me to want to prove him wrong, but his words also pushed me away. The criticism from my father regarding my pregnancy drove me deeper into troubled places I didn't yet recognize. I struggled with forming healthy intimate relationships. I thought I was choosing men who were vested in me. However, I chose men whose characteristics were opposite my father's. Instead, my choices found me in relationships with men who took advantage of me and misused and abused me.

My friends began to challenge my behavior and my choices. So then, I started asking myself, "Why had I experienced these things in my life? Why was I so angry, angry with myself, angry with my father? Why did I think sex was a superpower?

I began to participate in self-therapy. I wanted a male therapist, someone older. He was white (Caucasian) and wore a toupee (wig) and colorful tropical shirts. His office was comfortable, and the lighting was low. The big picture window also provided natural light. He provided a safe space to explore the years leading up to that point in my life. I learned (throughout my life) to devalue myself and be more tolerant of the man in my life. I learned how the "Superwoman Complex" reinforced my lack of self-trust, let alone others. More importantly, I learned how the sexual trauma, feelings of abandonment, and criticism from my father (in such an important stage in my life) reinforced toxic shame.

Although the memories of that day with my cousins are permanent and altering, the combined events throughout my life were present in my thoughts. I don't remember how I felt. Compliance is what comes to mind. Every direction or order was abided by without question. The damage it created became more evident as I provided therapeutic services to others. My client's descriptions of their situations triggered the realization of how those moments in my life broke down any framework to manage and maintain healthy relationships. My client's disclosure of their encounters with disrespect and abuse triggered my own experiences. Listening to others explore their behaviors, activities, or challenges would reinforce the toxic patterns created from previous life encounters. Over time, these stories intertwined with mine. I became fixated on the effects of the lacking.

When I think of what's lacking, I become overwhelmed with thoughts and questions, starting with my father and his role in my life. Although we are now in a better place in our relationship, I would question why my father wasn't who I would run to talk with when searching for understanding. I was angry, bitter, and resentful, and I would question why my brothers appeared to have the better parts of him. I was his firstborn and his only girl. Why didn't he protect me? Why didn't he warn me? Why did I feel left alone to figure it out? I questioned if he even loved me.

Fathers play a vital role in the lives of their children. I would say an even more prominent role in their daughter's lives. While all relationships have troubling moments, the father/daughter relationship is vital for a woman. Why? Because it aids in becoming the woman we are in the present and future. Fathers and daughters move throughout their lifetimes, and some are entirely unaware of forming unhealthy relationships between them. This may be attributed to generations of patterns within our families. These can be identified as absent, sexual abuse, emotionally unavailable, overly critical fathers who simultaneously host several families, and those dealing with addictions. These patterns are developed over generations causing fathers to lack insight into or ignore their behavior. However, these patterns affect their daughter's ability to form realistic and healthy expectations, including boundaries, and groom them to continue accepting the toxic traits within themselves and others.

I imagine this illusional wall acting as a protectant when I think of boundaries. It's that kind of wall that others can't see, but we, as individuals, know it is there. It's an individual force field used to protect one against harm. This protectant grows with us as we grow. Boundaries are defined as a person's borders, edging, or framing. Boundaries help manage and reinforce the working relationships within a physical and mental space, amongst others. They give us the freedom to exercise our morality and values within those relationships. They provide the fortitude to act when we are uncomfortable or satisfied within our space. Boundaries can be deliberately or instinctively established. The therapist in me pondered the development of these said boundaries. Why do they play such a small yet significant role in our lives?

(Author's note: I respect written and unwritten confidentiality agreements. Therefore, I am not revealing any personal client information throughout this chapter, M. Oliver).

Over the last several years of my practice and research, I have theorized that boundaries are one of the main ingredients to our foundation of healthy relationships. But first, we must understand how boundaries are developed. Boundaries present themselves at different stages of life; for example, babies are born with total trust that they are safe. They are not born with the innate awareness of danger, representing their innocence. Instead, they trust they will be fed, cleaned, clothed, and fall asleep without fear. Infants learn if they cry, they will receive rewarding experiences of nurturing and love because of their wants and needs.

Toddlers learn through interactions with their caregivers and other members of their community. This may include siblings, relatives, childcare centers, and churches. Boundaries continue to be reinforced in youth through friendships, extra-curricular activities, schools, and other authority figures. Relationships continue to form, change, and become more meaningful as we grow through adolescence and adulthood. For women, this can be a critical phase of our lives. And those individuals who are closest to us will influence our morals and values, ultimately impacting boundaries.

Some young girls were taught to be confident in saying "No." Others are taught that waving the pointed finger means, "you don't say NO to me." "Hush your mouth, child… BE CAREFUL with the words you choose… your mouth is too slick… Don't close that door or any doors in my house." Some young girls remember the unwanted feelings and emotions from being forced to sit uncomfortably on an Uncle's lap. We learned the behavior of being pleasing to the eyes that stare upon us. As little girls, we learned (or were taught) to be attentive to those close to us and those we "love." As a result, some are discouraged from expressing themselves. Many witness patterns of abuse. Some of us may have been ignored or left alone.

Women have shared (with me) their personal experiences about their relationships with their fathers and other loved ones. My pandora's box includes stories of women being abandoned and abused. Women of various ages share stories of their fathers, leaving them feeling unwanted and abandoned. Fathers beat their mothers sometimes to the point of being unrecognizable. I have empathized through stories of young girls and women touched inappropriately without their consent to take the place of their mothers in satisfying their fathers. Others repeat derogatory names that abusers call them over time, such as stupid, ugly, or bitch. Young ladies have shared the frustration and sadness of watching their fathers prioritize their girlfriends and offer gifts to barter forgiveness from their daughters.

These childhood experiences shape us significantly. The effects can be pretty damaging. Most women, including myself, have shared experiences of not knowing how to establish healthy boundaries. Therefore, we create unhealthy relationship boundaries between ourselves and others. Clinicians identify these unhealthy boundaries in two different categories, rigid and porous. Having rigid boundaries may be identified as: 'One who has challenges with being emotionally available.' They keep others at a distance. These would be women who may struggle with close relationships, including their children, significant others, co-workers, or anyone she would interact with daily. Women who have difficulty saying "no" would be illustrated as having a porous use of boundaries. They are seekers of acceptance. Women who fit within this category are more apt to follow through with the appeasement of others, even if it doesn't feel good.

Women who struggle with setting boundaries (typically) live with unrecognizable feelings of shame. Shame is a painful feeling of humiliation or distress caused by the consciousness of not living up to our own standards or other people's standards. Shame is an emotion we hold within. This strong emotion teaches us how to adapt to our family, friends, work environments, and other social groups. Shame shapes our values and teaches us the do's and don'ts, which is healthy for everyone. However, shame can also cause us to feel pain and fear. These emotions are created by surroundings that maintain abuse and neglect. We harbor shame when our environment doesn't support our real needs.

When we experience intense, strong feelings of shame, it influences our response to other people and situations. Shame or guilt focuses on your character as an individual, and it becomes incredibly toxic when it starts to affect your sense of self. This effect will hang around your every existence, causing a constant cycle of negative thoughts, leaving you to feel pessimistic about everyday life. This ongoing loop of negative thinking patterns infects your view of self, brewing into toxic shame.

Past experiences of abuse, and emotionally neglectful parenting, aids in developing shame. Parents play a vital role in normalizing mistakes and teaching their children about the consequences of their actions or behavior. Nonetheless, some parents may send harmful messages that could impact their child's personalities. When the needs are not acknowledged and acted upon, individuals may internally struggle with judgment, self-worth, and moods, like depression and anxiety—toxic shame and the constant feeling that you are worthless. According to the renowned researcher from the University of Houston, Brene Brown, shame is an intensely painful feeling or experience of believing that we are flawed and, therefore, unworthy of love and belonging. It happens when other people treat you poorly, and you turn that treatment into a belief about yourself. Childhood and adolescent years can leave a person most vulnerable to toxic shame.

The challenge with toxic shame is that it creates unhealthy conditions and maintains the negative messages of your trauma. It substantially ignites an emotional state where it becomes a catalyst for isolation or disengagement within the present moment. This is called a trigger. Triggers occur when you experience an event that reminds you of a past encounter or memory. For instance, imagine you and your significant other are out at a fancy restaurant, escorted into a room with yellow wallpaper, and the house special is fried fish. You notice brewing feelings of irritability and agitation. The conversation with your partner becomes full of sarcasm. You complain about how the food and evening are terrible. You demand to bring the night to a close. Your partner is baffled and confused. You are being repeatedly asked, "What is bothering you?" You are unable to answer. You are unaware that the wallpaper unconsciously reminds you of when your grandmother had her 4th Friday Fish Fries. The yellow walls and the smell of fish frying places you back to the 6-year-old child and your grandmother's kitchen. It's the same place where your grandfather made it his business to touch you inappropriately.

Triggers can be unconscious or conscious. Many bury their experienced trauma, trying to forget through suppression. Others cannot help but remember pieces of life's memories we have repressed over the years. The shame associated with these memories can hold great pain and feelings of inadequacy. However, in each instance, defense mechanisms develop. Defenses are behaviors individuals create to protect themselves from reexperiencing unpleasant feelings or events. These control mechanisms consist of perfectionism, aggression, or righteousness. As a result, some may bury themselves in work, addictions or obsessions may develop. Others build low self-esteem and become co-dependent. The challenge with low self-esteem is its roots in diminishing self-love. When self-love is not present, individuals grow suicidal thoughts and develop suicidal behavior.

The use of defense mechanisms is natural. However, many of us do not recognize when we are using them. While defense mechanisms seem to protect, they can also create harm caused by overusing this self-protection impulse. This may create a breakdown in essential relationships with our children, our significant other, and most

133

importantly ourselves. They impact our social skills allowing for healthy interaction with co-workers, neighbors, or friends. We find ourselves putting in long hours at work or missing major events in the lives of our loved ones and creating challenges in communicating with others. Physical and psychological stress affects defense mechanisms placing them in overdrive and influencing our physical health. In adults, the psychological stress of our mistakes may have long-lasting negative results. The inability to repair or admit to past mistakes may affect or influence the growth of toxic shame.

Toxic shame filters the mind with negative messages. It has you believing you are stupid, incapable, and unlovable. These thoughts are untrue and have you seeing them as permanent. Toxic shame works to control different aspects of your life. First, toxic shame can isolate you, causing you to avoid or withdraw from others. You worry that you may hurt those around you based on your actions or choices. Emotional distress can come from different people, places, or things. The most common factor is negative self-talk, which generates undesirable emotions such as anger, embarrassment, worry, and fear.

It may also create a feeling of perfectionism. Perfectionism creates an overwhelming need for you to avoid showing vulnerability to prevent criticism. Finally, toxic shame can make it challenging to form relationships. The feeling of shame or guilt (programs) makes you think you are not worthy of love. It makes you uncomfortable to lower your guard with those you love. It also contributes to relationship tension. It causes you to be less receptive to constructive criticism or less empathetic toward those you love. The criticism reminds you of previous years of being shamed and emphasizes your thoughts of shortcomings. Criticism may provoke defensiveness and cause you to lash out at your partner, display dishonest behavior, or shut down emotionally. Today, this defensiveness in relationships with others and, most importantly, we (ourselves) have caused many women to take on the world alone.

Many women, specifically black women, have embraced this concept of taking on traumas alone to protect ourselves. We have been doing this for generations. Some would argue that culturally we were forced into this mode of coping. Historically, black women developed into being the rock of our communities. Throughout my career and learning more about myself regarding my issues with my father and trauma, I am better suited to recognize the unhealthy patterns I chose to live my life. I acknowledge my lack of boundaries and the toxic traits I developed from the shame festering within me. I'm able to identify my defense mechanisms to keep me safe. But there is still one defense mechanism that I must explore with you that I feel many of us share. We have adopted this "Superwoman" philosophy toward life. Our collective traumas and upbringing have shaped us to believe we can wear the invisible cloak with a big, bold, glittered "S" on our chest. We endure trauma, stress, societies expectations, and we struggle with saying "No." As a result, our relationships fail, our children struggle, and we face health challenges.

Countless women live by the idea that "we must do it all." Have the best careers while multitasking with family, home, exercise, and other tasks. This multitasking stretches us thin, all while neglecting ourselves in an effort to be perfect. Why do we embark on living our lives this way? We share this idea of having the responsibility to present an image of strength. We are compelled to suppress our emotions! We display resistance to being vulnerable in intimate relationships. We share a drive to succeed despite limited resources. There is an overwhelming need and obligation to help others. It has become the Black Woman's unspoken oath to manage stress and crown ourselves with resilience.

Today, strength includes being a mother, a professional, a wife or significant other, a homemaker, a teacher, a provider, a best friend, a community organizer, a daughter, and a sister. For some, every one of these roles is achieved within a 24-hour day, every day of the week. Women feel as though they must be strong. Some feel it is essential to maintain this image of strength because of our foremother's challenges. The expectations of society (even relationships) play into the need to maintain a strong black woman persona.

As young girls, we are raised in families, taught in schools, and watch television shows that perpetuate the need to maintain a high vitality level. Women have sat before me during coaching sessions discovering and learning how to feel again. The Superwoman Complex has stifled our ability to express ourselves and recognize emotions.

We struggle with internalizing our emotions, creating difficulties in nurturing our dearest relationships. This may imply that some of us are challenged to nurture our children or partners. Communication becomes a task that is avoided based on emotions. Feelings are synonymous with weakness, therefore creating unnecessary tension. I even recognize the complexity of asking for and accepting assistance or support. Early trauma provides lessons of vulnerability. The understanding became hurt, and defensive countermeasures were required to protect. However, the opposition with enduring vulnerability is having trouble not taking the lead and creating challenges in our intimate relationships. It then becomes an issue of control which generates anxiety and or depression.

Success becomes the motivation for freedom despite inadequate resources. This level of ambition drives a sense of pride in women who have lived with abuse or neglect. The mindset is that this level of freedom can only be obtained through consistent hard work. The need to achieve "the best" is to become the first person in the family to acquire a college education, make a six-figure salary, retire at 55, own a home (s), or provide for their children. Many women are working to obtain these goals without the support of family, partners, or their children's fathers. The burdensome weight of being the BEST creates a sense of pressure and guilt for those tirelessly working towards triumphs.

Early abuse, specifically sexual abuse, may limit the development of boundaries. Girls are said to have a genuine attribute to nurture others.

Abuse influences this ideal to its sufferers that they are least important, therefore, supporting a pleasing or passive personality. Research suggests that women with the 'Superwoman Syndrome' share a duty to assist others. In short, they wrestle with saying "No" and will commit to taking on multiple tasks and roles. Women show responsibility to meet the needs of others. They will overcommit themselves. This level of dedication provides a sense of use, honor, and gratification. However, in this case, loyalty can create breeding grounds for avoidance and solitude.

Many of us knowingly embrace the 'Superwoman Syndrome' to learn self-sufficiency to prevent or control future pain. It has become our motivation, our coping mechanism to "get by." Our mothers and grandmothers taught us to manage stress as best as possible. However, this syndrome creates discord in interpersonal relationships, stress-related health behaviors, and embodiments of stress.

Girls who have experienced trauma endured by those closest to them can create lifelong emotional challenges. Early life traumas result from low self-esteem, substance use, depression, and anxiety. Our relationships with our significant others, children, parents, and most importantly, ourselves are most impacted. Over the years, I have learned that the only way to heal is to no longer ignore it. Stop stuffing the experience. If you are ready to start your healing journey, a few things must occur. For starters, the commitment must be made to yourself that you bare down and fight your way through when things get complicated, thus requiring levels of vulnerability. Vulnerability is challenging because it requires you to be honest with yourself and those you love, regardless of how difficult it may be.

You must understand this process involves the mind, body, and soul and creating a network that supports healing. Get comfortable in learning to ask for help. Your state of mind may require that you seek assistance from a therapist, a professional, certified and trained specifically to address your specific needs. The body requires you to learn to embrace self-care and have an accountability partner. Self-care may include improving eating habits, attending medical and dental appointments, and exercising. What we feed our body influences our mood and thoughts. Lastly, feed your soul. Feeding your soul may come from attending church, support groups, or reading inspirational, motivational, or spiritual content. Spiritual sources are multidimensional and personal. Most importantly, know that this healing process will be difficult and painful. You will be required to facilitate and create change, but the emergence will be worth it!

You are a QUEEN; wear your CROWN with confidence and dignity!

Maquira Oliver, LMSW-C

ABOUT THE AUTHOR

MAQUIRA OLIVER

Hello good people! My name is Maquira Oliver. I want to take a few moments to introduce myself to you. I am a licensed clinical social worker practicing within the greater Detroit area. It has been my mission to service at-risk populations within the Black community. I began my career while in high school, volunteering in homeless shelters. In 2001, I obtained my bachelor's degree from Oakland University in Rochester, Michigan, majoring in sociology, focusing on social work. In 2010, I received my Mastered Degree from Wayne State University in Detroit, Michigan. I furthered my education by obtaining full licensing as a Clinical Social Worker.

My first paid experience was within the field of foster care. From there, I transitioned into mental health. I have dedicated at least 20 years to servicing children, families, men, and women from various walks of life.

I currently work with the MDHHS, Walter Reuther Psychiatric Hospital, as a Clinical Social Worker. I also established a private practice, Growing Well Clinical Therapy Services (GWCTS). In my clinical practice, I assist individuals between the ages of 16 - 99 with gaining a more fulfilled life. I aid in better managing symptoms of ADHD/ADD, Depression, Anxiety, Posttraumatic Stress Disorder, some personality disorders, and challenges with adjusting to changes and phases of life, to name a few. In addition, I provide mentorship and supervision to practicing limited licensed social workers within my practice. In addition to GWCTS, I partnered with the Black Therapist Support Network of Detroit, where my partner and I are devoted to building strong support for minority clinicians in the mental health community within metro Detroit.

I have made many unfortunate choices throughout my life journey and faced severe challenges. It took me years to accept my gifts and learn to love myself. Now a mother of three, a daughter, sister to my "Little-big" brothers, and friend. I have learned to embrace the challenges experienced throughout my life and identify them as steppingstones. These steppingstones led me to be the clinician I am today. I service my clients with integrity and dignity in the hopes that they, too, can identify their path of steppingstones to a more fulling and fruitful life.

Many blessings!
Maquira Oliver, LMSW
Licensed Master Clinical Social Worker
Cell: 734-846-5723
growingwellclinical@gmail.com and blacktherapistdetroit@gmail.com

CHAPTER TEN

Trust No One?

BY BRENDA WARREN

The first man I ever loved, who told me he loved me too, was tall, dark, and handsome. His six-foot-two-inch muscular frame was the envy of many. His smile was a chick magnet and would often stop men and women in their tracks. When he spoke, his deep voice filled the room. His singing was world-class. He displayed his gift often in nightclubs or prisons, depending on his location at the time. In church, his gospel singing changed people's lives. This charismatic well-dressed man was in his thirties when he married my seventeen-year-old love-struck mother—a young woman with her own daddy-daughter issues.

As the oldest child with two younger brothers produced from this volatile union, I witnessed more than I will ever discuss here or anywhere else. My father was a complicated man. One minute he was the love of my life. The next, he was Satan incarnate. Prone to fits of anger, seemly for no reason, within minutes, he would love the family and me as if we were God's gift to his world. The problem was I never knew which version of him would show up. I learned early; that life is a battlefield. I dodged or knew where to hide during and after the subsequent explosion. It became a way of life for my little brothers and me. This beautiful nightmare I called my father would shape how I viewed men, God, and the world in general.

Daddy's love me, hate me behavior caused a roller coaster of emotions. I never knew if I would be considered worthy of his time from one day to the next. I learned to be a chameleon adapting to the whims of his personality shifts to gain his approval. My relationship with my father

141

would lay the groundwork for some very dysfunctional interactions with the men in my life. My walk with Christ would be challenging due to how my earthly father figure presented himself. My earthly father's example of how a father treated me led me to think God was the same. It would take years for me to believe God was not like man.

By the time I joined the military, I trusted no one. I feared abandonment and became a significant people pleaser with unhealthy boundaries having no limits. I went along to get along because my self-esteem was low. I would go on to have many unsuccessful relationships and marriages. Three marriages and three divorces, to be exact. It would be years before I gained my sense of worthiness. Self-worth, self-love, self-confidence, and personal development, to become unapologetically unstoppable, would require a journey filled with soul searching.

Joining the Marine Corps was my ticket to going to places I had only imagined. It was also an attempt to leave behind the war zone during my childhood. In my twenty years of service, I got everything I imagined and more than I had thought possible. I walked through the land mines of life with many battle scars. Most of my scars are invisible to the naked eye, with the worst created during my military service. Only a select few have been deemed worthy of being shown the shrapnel left embedded in my soul. Some have betrayed that trust and have been cut off without warning. Others still hold their place of honor.

At this moment, I will share with you a small view from my past, kept locked away until now:

The blood that splashed across my face came from my mother's nose. Daddy had slapped her once again. I was three or four years old. Their daily fights were epic and a part of our everyday life in my home. Mommy almost dropped my new baby brother (Bruce) at that time. My other brother (Junior) was hiding in the corner, as always. I could still hear my father cursing as he went upstairs. Momma cleaned us up and sat on the steps to smoke a cigarette. While we were sitting on the cold concrete stairs, she told me never to be with a man that hits me.

Unfortunately, I repeated her pattern. As she continued to speak that night, it was clear that would be the last time my dad got away with hitting my mother without a response. Their brawls escalated from there until one summer day that changed everything.

It was Friday. Daddy got paid, and he always came home drunk. I was five years old. As my brothers and I played and danced to the music, Momma was cooking as she spoke with my aunt. I overheard my mother tell my aunt she was not in the mood for my father's mess today. Later that evening, he arrived home drunk, as usual, with treats for my brothers and me. Mommy was at the stove. It did not take long before their voices began to rise.

Momma asked about the rent money. When she did, my father slapped her hard across her face and began to shake her. He let loose a long list of profanity and ungrateful comments. He pushed Momma to the floor and turned to walk away. Mommy got up, grabbed the cast iron frying pan, and began beating him in the head.

I still remember the sound it made to this day, even with the loud music playing in the background. Daddy fell to the floor; blood was all around him. Momma dropped the pan and told me to take the boys upstairs. I did as I was told. She called Uncle Freddy and 911. "I think I finally killed him she said," as she headed to her favorite smoking spot, waiting for everyone to arrive, he laid motionless on the floor.

We moved in with my uncle that day. Daddy was in the hospital for a while. When he got out of the hospital, he came to get my brothers and me. We got to stay with him for a long time before he took me back to mom and kept the boys. It would be a while before I discovered my father had taken us without permission.

The worst thing of all was finding out he did not want me. I heard him tell my grandmother I was too much like my mother. As I look back, I remember the pain of feeling rejected. The fear of abandonment and feelings of not being worthy were well planted. Those emotions in later years would keep me in relationships well past their expiration. When my mom finally got my brothers back, she moved us to Augusta, Georgia, to live with my Uncle Glenn until she could afford our place. After that, my father became a ghost in our lives as he raised another family with my stepmom, Shirley.

My father would occasionally call, promising to come to see me and assuring me he would always be there to protect me. My grandmother, Daddy's mother, requested I spend the summer in Delaware, as I had trouble adjusting to our new surroundings. Spending time in Deleware would be great because I could see my father and work with my dad at the gas station.

I wanted desperately for my daddy to want me. I promised myself I would do whatever it took to get daddy to love me like he loved Shirley's kids. Then maybe he would keep me too. I paid attention and figured out everything he liked. I wanted his approval and looked for ways to make him want me. I began looking for things that would make my daddy proud of me became an obsession. Reflecting, I realized it was a behavior I am sad to say I took into my adult relationships. I developed a habit of doing whatever it took to gain acceptance. I would give and give in my relationships to gain approval. It took a while for me to learn you can not give someone more of what they already don't appreciate to make them love you.

My desire to please my dad was never more evident than when we played the game called "catch me." Every day I would crawl up on top of the soda machine and yell, "catch me, daddy." Daddy would reach out his arms and catch me, giving me a big hug. One day I yelled, "catch me, daddy," Daddy reached out his arms, I jumped, and he pulled them back. I hit the concrete floor. Crying with a bloody nose, my dad looked down at me and said, "Big girls, don't cry and don't trust anybody but yourself, especially not a man." That day I learned not to trust. It took two months of scraped knees before I yelled, "look, daddy!" and jumped off that soda machine, landing on my own two feet. My dad picked me up, gave me a big hug, and said, good girl. After that, I never let him see me cry again, or anyone else, for that matter.

I had his approval again. I knew I didn't need anyone to catch me ever again; I was five years old when I made that decision. I would learn about the boogie man and why my dad told me not to trust anyone but myself by year's end.

When I returned to Georgia to be with Momma, we had our own place. Momma's new boyfriend gave me the creeps; he lived with us. He was a big fat man that was always eating. He and Momma were a perfect fit because she loved to cook and was good at it. Both my brothers learned to cook as well as our Momma. I cook but not with the joy Momma had. Cooking was a duty to me growing up because Momma worked two jobs, and I was responsible for feeding my brothers. I would tell her when I grow up, I will have enough money for a chef and live in a big house. Momma would smile and say I believe you will have one someday, baby. Momma always encouraged us to dream big.

In the meantime, I was stuck in the little house with the second man to teach me why I should trust no one. It started with him having me sit on his lap. In no time, this man would steal my innocence. The monster in the house had daily access to me every time Momma went to work. He convinced me that no one would love me if I told anyone, and he would kill my family and me. Worst of all, that man convinced my young mind that God did not love me.

Living lies now became the pattern for the little girl lost and left with the only escape I had, my imagination. To this day, my mind and body can be in many different places at one time, thanks to what I call the gift of my imagination. Thanks to my imagination, the gift that keeps on giving, I maintained my sanity.

I learned never to leave an opening for the enemy in the Marines. Any breach must be dealt with quickly, and the same mistake could cost you your life. So, I learned my lessons well. But, unfortunately, maybe I learned my lessons too well as I shut out the world and trapped myself in a never-ending battle with myself.

The struggle to NEVER lose control and always have a plan A thru Z is exhausting. But, like Captain James T. Kirk of Star Trek fame, "I had my Kobe-ashe-marue escape route well planned and ready to execute at any moment." My creed: "trust no one; failure is not an option. It's a choice, and always have a way out." Having that creed, I lived always waiting for the other shoe to drop, believing I controlled the shoe. However, I could not have anticipated a hairline crack in my armor would spin my world out of control in more ways than one.

I waited for my father or God to come to save me. Neither one showed up. I have always known during times of pure hell; that many others would have fallen into the bottomless pit of despair, never to return. Yet somehow, I kept going even after three real-life attempts at suicide and years of continual thoughts on the subject. There has got to be a purpose greater than I know for the continued resilience of my mind despite the many attacks that never seem to stop coming.

Years of repeated sexual harassment and three sexual assaults during my time in the service led me down a destructive path. My stay in the psychiatric ward would leave me suicidal and feeling genuinely worthless. In my world, "Marines don't do that." I worked hard to hide the hurt, sense of betrayal, and shame I felt from my fellow team members. I spiraled deeper and deeper with each attack while numbing my pain with drugs and alcohol. I could not tell my family what was happening. My parents did not want me to enter the military service.

I was expected to attend college for Business Management. My mother picked out the school. My entry into the marines required my mother's signature due to my age. At the permission signing, my mother told me, "If I sign this paper, you better never complain about what they do to you, and you better retire. Do you understand me?" Yes, ma'am, was my reply. I retired as a Gunnery Sergeant after 20 years of active service honorably. Momma was so proud of me, bragging to all her friends and anyone who would listen. My mother would go to her grave, never knowing the horrors I endured during my time in the military.

The discovery by my military command of my alcohol and prescription drug addictions is what led to my reconnection with my father. I spent months in the military drug and alcohol program learning to deal with my issues drug-free. My first marriage had become physically abusive and was all but over. Fearing for my life, I requested relocation orders to move closer to my family. Soon after completing treatment, I was transferred to Quantico, Virginia, for continued rehabilitation.

My father stepped up to the plate during the brink of my first divorce. I was also on the path of losing my military career. Building our relationship was slow, complex, and sometimes very painful. But, for the first time in my life, I knew my father loved me and was in for the long haul to support me through this process as I headed through sobriety. I had blamed my father for ALL sexual abuse, my inability to trust a man, and my anger issues. I felt he failed as a father when he did not protect me from being abused.

My mother had instructed me never to tell my father or grandmother what happened when we lived in Georgia. She called it the incident. My mother said she would lose custody of my brothers and me if they knew. Once again, an adult wanted me to keep their secret. That was a lot of pressure to place on a child. When the abuse was discovered, we moved back close to my father. Not wanting to be why my mother lost us (kids), I kept my mouth shut. I stopped talking for a while. Momma called it my quiet year. To this day, I don't like keeping secrets.

It would be years of professional counseling and prayer before I could let go of the anger I held for my mother and father. Momma's denial of the incident would forever damage our ability to communicate. I deemed my father a failure and not worthy of forgiveness.

My Aunt Elaine, my father's sister, was my one trusted confidant, and even she did not know the real me. I will be forever grateful to God for a second chance that opened my heart to my parents before they died. Over the years before his death, we (my father) developed a very loving relationship that forged a strong enough connection that I could feel his presence.

Although our relationship was indeed robust and total trust was an elusive friend. I had developed the ability to wear the mask. I would let someone in just enough to maintain a relationship, yet I always waited for them to betray my trust. After my relationship ended, it would be years before I entered a relationship again. We had been friends for over ten years.

Our friendship was not enough to sustain the relationship. After five years of military deployment, combined with my low self-esteem, my lack of trust, and my anger issues, my relationship ended. I felt that was the worst part of my life.

It took three days and six flights before I arrived at the hospital, where my father lay in a coma. I was a United States Marine stationed in Okinawa, Japan, at Camp Forster when I received the call. My dad had an aneurysm explode in his head in Wilmington, Delaware. I was notified he had passed, but I knew that was not true because I could still feel him. So, I would not contact my family until I reached the hospital. We were close by now, and I knew he would wait for me no matter how long it took me to get there.

I arrived late in the evening. My brother met me in front of the hospital. The look on his face was one of relief. He said, "dad is waiting for you;

he is brain dead. His heart is still beating. They wanted us to pull the plug. Aunt Elaine made them wait on you." Aunt Elaine and my brother had taken turns telling my dad I was coming until I arrived. Later, she told me how his monitors would blink whenever he heard my name. I entered the room to find him attached to many monitors. He was flanked by my mother and stepmother, both crying. My grandmother, daddy's mother, sat quietly in the corner; my Aunt Elaine, daddy's sister, stood by her side. No one said a word.

One monitor was a flat line. One tracked brain activity; the other monitored blood pressure and heartbeat, as his heart was slow and faint. I slowly approached the bed and reached for his hand. With his hand firmly held in mine, I said, "It's ok, daddy, you can go now. I am here. I love you." I watched tears begin to fall from his eyes. The monitors start to beat faster, and then slowly, they all flat-lined. He was gone.

My two moms and grandmother began to wale as nurses and doctors flooded the room, confirming what everyone already knew; daddy crossed over to the other side. My brother paced and went to comfort our mother. I kept my stepmother from falling to the floor. Aunt Elaine cried silently as she tried to comfort grandmother. A thousand emotions filled my mind as we left the cold building. I knew that the father I had just begun to understand would no longer be here to finish answering all the remaining questions.

I would soon be divorced for the second time. This ending would cause me to seek God like never before. I began to read the Bible to develop a personal relationship I had never had before. I would spend years knowing what it meant to serve God. When I entered my third marriage with a Christian man, I thought this was it. I have finally found my life partner. Two weeks after my wedding, I knew I had made the biggest mistake of my life. I would spend my entire marriage trying to make it work.

I did not want another divorce. In 2011, I was diagnosed with Post Traumatic Stress Disorder (PTSD) and Military Sexual Trauma (MST).

I was filled with shame, and I did not tell my husband, family, co-workers, or friends. By 2013 I had a complete mental breakdown. I had to leave my job as a Hospital Administrator. I stepped down from all of my Board of Directors positions within my community. I would remain motionless on my couch for eight years, gaining weight. I would still be helping others live their best life during that time, as mine was in shambles. I still wanted my hallmark moment. Unfortunately, that would not be the case, as I would find myself divorced for the third time after twenty-three years of marriage.

A prayer would finally get me off the couch in 2019. Walking in my driveway daily as I talked to God, I lost sixty-five pounds while making videos. My, Tell Yourself Tuesday videos were viewed around the world. I hit total rock bottom in July 2020 when I realized my husband was not coming back. The pain was so devastating that I found myself on the national crisis hotline holding a medication bottle. The gentleman on the other end of the line convinced me to take one pill and get some rest. He asked me to find something to do that would keep me busy. My child Alex was away at college, and my husband was gone. It was just my three Guinea Pigs and me.

Over the next eighteen months, I would get professional counseling to help me deal with my daddy-daughter issues, post-traumatic stress, military sexual trauma, and how to have healthy relationships. Finally, my third divorce became final, and my relationships with my ex-husbands were friendly.

I developed the TAPIN Method, authored my first book, created courses, became a Mental Fitness Coach, TV Host, started my own YouTube Channel, and spoke all over the world, all from the comfort of my own home. I take every other month off because I need it for good mental health.

I started learning how to trust others when my father reentered my life. Now, I am learning to trust myself and the choices I make. I teach others how to build trust over time with their significant other. Also, they can build confidence in adult friendships, at the workplace, or with other family members.

I finally understand that trust is the foundation of all great relationships - whether between family or friends. When both sides of each relationship have trust, people are more open and likely to spend more time with each other. Having trust in someone means you trust that you can go to the other person and rely on them. Trust was a new concept for me as I always relied on myself.

Letting go of past hurts was critical in reclaiming my life and removing the limiting beliefs that no one could be trusted, not even God. The trust was gone. As my faith has deepened, I am thankful that God is not like man. I am grateful my earthly father and I worked toward a healthy relationship before he passed. I have decided to love like there is no heartbreak as I help others live unapologetically unstoppable lives. Here are three things you can do to build trust with another person today:

- **Keep agreements and promises.** When you keep your promises, you show the other person they can depend on you! This is a crucial foundation of trust. If an agreement or promise is broken, there should always be an open line of communication explaining why.
- **Listen without judgment.** Create an environment where the people around you feel heard. Instead of judging someone for what they share with you, try to understand where they are coming from or feeling. Be sure to give them a nod to show them you are engaged and present.
- **Share.** Be curious about those around you and be willing to open yourself up as well. **Trust will naturally build as people feel like they know you better.**

Preserving the pain of my past did not serve me. I had to let it go!! **Today, I know who I am, what I want, and what is suitable for me.**

I am building up my inner strength to follow what is true for me despite past traumas. I have the power to create my best life. I am determined to make it a love story with an epic adventure as I trust myself to make better choices.

Brenda Warren

ABOUT THE AUTHOR

BRENDA WARREN

Brenda Warren, The Solutionist, also known as Voice for the Voiceless, is a retired United States Marine, Author, Host of the show Talk To Me, Podcaster, and Mental Fitness Coach.

Brenda Warren grew up in Wilmington, DE as the oldest child with two younger brothers. Her mother, a serial entrepreneur, instilled in Brenda the value of hard work and choosing your own path.

Brenda's path would lead her to join the United States Marine Corps at age 17, 2 days after graduating from high school. In the military, she traveled the world and took leadership and professional development courses. Brenda would own and operated six different successful businesses during her twenty years on active duty before retiring in August of 2000 as a Gunnery Sergeant. In addition, Brenda studied coaching and began teaching men and women how to live a life on purpose.

After retirement, Brenda became a hospital administrator. She continued traveling the world, teaching others about leadership, self-care, cultivating healthy relationships, and spiritual growth until she was sidelined due to mental health reasons. While recovering, Brenda created The TAPIN Method™ (Transformation Announce Prepare Imagine Nurture) to help people transform their lives. Over the years, she has focused on women over 40, teaching them to live an unapologetic unstoppable life in private coaching groups. In addition, Brenda teaches Mental Fitness using a mind, body, and soul approach.

Brenda also conducts interviews on her show Talk To Me, helping Veterans, Entrepreneurs, and Authors turn their mess or mission into messages. She has been featured on various podcasts, magazines, The Best You TV Summit, and was the Host of The Brooklyn Cafe TV Show on The Editors Desk.

Brenda believes everyone has a story waiting to be told. She creates safe spaces for people to share their stories and learn how to remove barriers to living their best life using the TAPIN Method™

Today, Brenda empowers others to live unapologetically unstoppable lives. Brenda's passion is helping get the word out that living your best life is possible.

For additional information and support, check out Brenda at:

https://linktr.ee/brendathesoulutionist
Instagram: @brendathesoulutionist
YouTube: Brenda Warren or www.bit.ly/3s4FC7
LinkedIn: Brenda Warren

CHAPTER ELEVEN

The Father of Lies

BY TIFFANY "CrisTene" WASHINGTON

*Tell a lie once and all your truths become questionable. -**Unknown***

*Fathers, the way you raise your daughters determines if they will grow up to be someone's dream or someone's nightmare. – **Algernon Baker, Ph.D., LMFT***

Who is the *Father of Lies*? Well, for many, when we hear this phrase or idiom, we expeditiously think of other names such as Satan, Lucifer, the Devil, or the Evil One. In comparison, others may say, Leviathan, Beelzebub, Fallen Star, and many other monikers are associated. The imagery that one would possibly see is of a ghastly figure with horns, an elongated chin or face of wickedness and immorality, and that doltish pitchfork.

But whatever and whoever He is called or what illustration we give Him, we know that He is far from the representation of Truth, Honesty, or Integrity.

I had my own individual *Father of Lies*. He was my ***father*** who could possibly mirror those same images or adjectives that were influenced by Lucifer himself.

The *Father of Lies* influenced the lies that my ***father*** told me and what he did to me. Those same lies hurt me, pained me, and plagued me for years to come.

Yes! Me!

I, Tiffany "CrisTene" Washington, am a singer-songwriter and pianist, born and raised in Philadelphia, Pennsylvania.

I never blamed my parents or ***father*** for how I turned out.

I mean… I turned out pretty good, considering some of my trauma and circumstances. I was raised in Philly and went to Philadelphia's Creative and Performing Arts High School. There, I majored in vocal studies. Afterward, I graduated from Temple University with a bachelor's degree in Music. I am an active performer that started as an adolescent in Church to gain confidence or what I would call ***God-fidence.***[1]

So yeah, I guess I did well. Right?

Later, I completed my master's degree with a concentration in Public Health Administration and coursework for another master's in education. Now, I am a prospective law student.

Sounds really good! Right?

Wrong! While those overachieving acts may sound good, did you really read between the lies… I mean, lines of my questions of validation? Did you? Just joking. All those things are true about me. But, let me share more as you take this run (with me) down memory lane.

Although these are all true accomplishments, they may lead one to think or believe that I was ***not*** a victim of any circumstances or even a victim of trauma and pain. However, the juxtaposition of trauma and pain alongside the achievements haunted every area of my life. Hence, school was my outlet. Music was my medicine, and people were my magnets. Unfortunately, it was people who hurt me the most. Sound familiar? Typically, the abused becomes an abuser to others and/or a

---

[1] Confidence in God; Superior confidence because of the spirit of God on the inside of you. Coined by Author Jehyve Floyd (2021)

self-inflictor. They also tolerate more abuse, especially if they struggle with people-pleasing behavior.

People-pleasing behavior is very much self-inflicted abuse caused by a history of being abused. We, as people-pleasers, are usually very sacrificial. We want to make everybody happy. We want to become a personal lifesaver and put others' needs before our own. Now nothing can be wrong with that. Right? Correct! Except for one thing.

"People pleasers often think their behaviors are selfless, which is not always the case. People pleasers often expect others to respond with praise and appreciation for their sacrifice and tireless efforts. This gets problematic when their self-worth becomes dependent on others' opinions. When their actions are not met with the praise and appreciation they think they deserve; it causes frustration and resentment. These resentment damages relationships and can lead to tension and disconnection over time" (Standhart, 2021).

The people-pleaser becomes addicted to pain and abuse, which wreaks havoc in every area of their life, especially in relationships, more importantly, the intimate ones. In many cases, the people-pleasing personality correlates with fear of abandonment or rejection that resulted from abuse. Not to say that loving, praising, or helping people are wrong, but the level of expectation that comes out of it can be a detriment. God designed us to long for companionship as humans, but he also forewarns the same.

A man of many companions may come to ruin, but there is a friend who sticks closer than a brother. (Proverbs 18:24, ESV).

Two are better than one; because they have a good reward for their labour. For if they fall, the one will lift up his fellow: but woe to him that is alone when he falleth; for he hath not another to help him up. (Ecclesiastes 4:9-10, KJV).

This is considering the balance of your companions in your life. Some will tear you down into ruin, but there are ones that you will form a bond so deep that their love and loyalty will build you up. However, this is an individual journey that one has to work through on their own, with observation and experience. *You genuinely do not know who to have in your circle until you know who NOT to have in your circle.* And if you are a people pleaser, there will be more companions in your circle leading to ruin and causing demise than that friend who is like a brother. People pleasers do not always know when to set boundaries due to fear of rejection or being abandoned again. I say this again because it was a breach of boundaries that caused the people-pleasing behavior, resulting in weaker self-boundaries later.

God also designed us for intimate companionship.

Therefore, a man shall leave his father and his mother and hold fast to his wife, and they shall become one flesh. (Genesis 2:24, ESV)

Let marriage be held in honor among all, and let the marriage bed be undefiled, for God will judge the adulterer and all the sexually immoral. (Hebrews 13:4, ESV)

This is God's design for intimate companionship, meaning marriage. However, *people-pleasing* behavior and other personality flaws will impact these relationships too. And impact those relationships on a level you would have never thought or imagined. That is because an individual's trauma and life's issues will always show up elsewhere in their life. We all have some level of flaw or issues. If not, we would be perfect. Show me a person who doesn't have any issues, and I will show you a person who is a liar. #Periodt[2]

I grew up in the Christian Faith, which has created the very person you are listening to. I am not perfect, but I strive to live my life by the Word

---

[2] Hashtag used on social media to show that a statement is final. It defines a means of exclamation, shout and/or final word.

of God, which has also helped me in processing and healing from the childhood trauma that was inflicted upon me.

Interestingly, neither of my parents raised me in Church, but I decided to start going. We resided in the Logan section of Philadelphia for a bit, right off Old York Road and Courtland streets. There was a Church around the corner from me called *Faith Tabernacle*. I cannot remember the specific denomination or even the Pastor. The Church was located adjacent to one of the busiest streets in Philadelphia, Broad Street, and intersected with Belfield Avenue. On that corner was Sid Booker's, which always did have (and still has) the best shrimp baskets one could ever taste. Just thinking and writing about it creates a nostalgic moment during my elementary years. I remember my parents would go to Sid Booker's to get shrimp, and I would identify that Church.

One Sunday, my younger cousins and I walked to Church and sat through an entire service. I did it again and again and again after that. I can vaguely remember how I transitioned to the Church that I am currently a member of, 'Impacting Your World Christian Center.' That was my first independent decision to become who I have now become. I remember going to this Non-Denominational Church that had a timeless Youth Ministry that built my spirit man and added to my **Godfidence**. In Church, I sang and performed all the time, which helped me develop as a musician and a person who truly understood their musical gifts. I have God to thank and my aunt, who introduced me to that ministry. There, I grew and was able to get the Paternal love and longing from God and male role models (Pastors and ministry leaders) that I did not receive from my biological **father.**

Oh yeah, back to him. Back to the abuse and lies. My apologies for taking you on an enigmatic journey or conundrum. By now, you may have an idea of where this is headed.

My **father** was a Musician and an Army Veteran. According to my mother, he was "one of the *flyest* men she ever saw. He drove a Mercedes, wore Chinchilla coats, and had more gold than Trinidad James.[3] To me, he was the *dopest* guitarist who would play George Benson and Carlos Santana under the stage. I can honestly accredit him for my musical abilities and give him many other short-lived accolades and soon disregarded. He was my music idol until the day his violation would not allow me to see him as such any further. At such a young age, filled with disappointment, abandonment, neglect, rejection, and the breach of boundaries on my physical body as a child, that breach caused me and others so much pain. I can still hear the arguments between him and my mother. At times, I can still feel the heavy spirit in the home, as if I am still there. I still see the tears rolling down my mother's face. I still hear the conversations that I was not supposed to overhear, my mother crying and pleading to aunts and maybe her girlfriends for direction. But what I did not feel was protected by my *father,* as he once said he would. I no longer felt loved by him like he said he did. I no longer felt safe as he said he would keep me. And I no longer felt like *Daddy's little girl* but, shamefully, *Daddy's little woman.* Let that sink in…....

There was a deep disdain in my soul to get away and stay away from him. Too painful, so I digress. Please turn the page and change the scene.
Lights! Camera! Action!
I pick up the microphone and got on stage to perform.
Feet were cold but Palms were sweaty and warm.
Take your time "Tiff" I hear from the crowd
After the first note I sang the cheering grew loud
Note after note
Step after step
This gets so much easier
Ard I'm done, so "Cut the check[4]"!

-CrisTene ♫

---

[3] Trinidadian-America Rapper known for his hit single "All Gold Everything" released in 2012 and held Billboard Hot 100 Chart status.
[4] Slang or vernacular meaning to "remit payment

This was the gradual sensation that I felt from being a beginning performer to being a next-level performer, and in the sample of Rapper Drake, "You can't get no freer Randy." I was now getting paid for performances, and this was not my first time, nor would it be my last. I grew more confidence, and as I stated before, **God-fidence**, and I finally recognized my talent's worth. But not just my talent's worth, but *Tiffany's* worth. "CrisTene's Worth." And just in case you cannot pronounce my legal middle name, which is also my pseudonym, it is phonetically **Kris-ten-aye**!!"

Say it right! Please and thank you.

Do you know what it took me to gain this God-fidence? It was not how long it took me but, most importantly, what it took from me. This *God-fidence* did not naturally occur and did not take work or labor. It took pain. One of my mentors, Prophetess Barbara L. McClary, told me it was called "Purpose-Driven Pain" (2016). This "purpose-driven pain was caused by...

You guessed it. Remember that *father of lies* that I mentioned? Yup! That guy.

The people-pleasing behavior came from being violated. At first, I was timid, and then I grew angry. Since anger is a product of pain, I can now understand why my emotions and temperament controlled my life. I did not understand the worth of my talent, let alone my worth as a woman or my worth as a Child of God. I allowed my performances and services to be "free and free, and then, free was **NOT** for me!" LOL.[5] I had to laugh because it was true. I feared being rejected and upsetting others by charging a price for my time and performances. I did not want to invite a stigma that I was overstepping other people's boundaries. However, the truth was that I was not putting any boundaries in place for myself!

---

[5] Acronym for Laugh out Loud (LOL). Typically used in texting

Authors Henry Cloud and John Townsend indicated (1992) that the fear of abandonment keeps many people from setting boundaries in the first place, as well as the fear of rejection. This causes an individual not to set solid boundaries for themselves or others. This causes a breach on either end or side. Furthermore, when trying to establish a boundary, there is a feeling of guilt. This is a lot to process, from the start of a childhood traumatic experience to not simply saying "no" because of a lack of self-worth and boundaries. The feelings of the first man I loved—my *father*—who did not seem to love me back, caused my life experiences to be filled with guilt. I felt that I was not deserving of compensation for my talents. Add insult to add injury, that anger and lack of temperance I exerted caused unresolved pain left in the depth of my soul.

I found relief in being very accomplished and overachieving. But this just buried the pain so that I did not have to process it or feel the guilt of an act that I knew was not my fault. I did not want to face the painful memories and past, but they still took root in my soul and contributed to my trust in people, specifically men, and the lack of confidence to leave my daughter with anyone. I was an overprotective mother with separation anxiety, not allowing my daughter to go anywhere without Mommy. My *self-made* and *self-proclamations* made me. Doing anything to become stronger, wiser, and better is what carried me through. But that still was not enough. I allowed people to hurt me, and I hurt people. The dormant anger inside me crept out at the most inopportune moments causing me to do things that I did not mean to do and say things that I did not mean to say.

Did I process my pain and heal suitably or not at all? After all the achievements were met, completed, and done, I still felt unresolved. My love and belief in God allowed me to heal to the point of forgiving, which many may say is the hardest part. *For if you forgive other people when they sin against you, your heavenly Father will also forgive you. (Matthew 6:14, NIV)*

Oddly, I forgave my *father*, but I learned later that I did not forgive my mother and did not forgive myself for a while. This was due to my empathic and people-pleasing nature, in which you love your abusers but don't love yourself. I did not hold any resentment towards my mother, but the pain of her leaving me with my *father* that night still haunted my thoughts. She knew he was not mentally well from the drug abuse and his own diagnosed psychoses, yet she still left me there alone.

My overachieving nature was a trauma response in order for me to feel worthy and wanted. But I did not realize that resolution to the pain from the trauma was the key to healing and true freedom from the emotional prison of my heart and mind. God sustained me through my adolescent and teenage years and helped me forgive and not be bitter or hateful.

I attended Church services, heard sermons, and read the Word to assist me with getting to a place of forgiving my *father*. Finally, I could talk to him and even acknowledge him, but until this day, it is difficult for me to tell him that I love him. Honestly, it is not that I don't. But it feels like a justification of his violation if I were to tell him. We can connect on some life levels but mainly with Music. It took over twenty years to get to that point, and it is still progressing. However, I am uncertain if the full capacity of trust can be repaired. This trust breach led me onto a destructive journey with the men I chose for relationships. But we can discuss that at another time, in another chapter, or maybe in another book.

These men that I dated also abused me in one way or another. If they were not physically abusive, they were mentally, emotionally, or verbally. I realized that I was also an empath. An empath's nature is to love their abuser and become addicted to the abuse or pain. Why? Due to the repeated pain of rejection and/or people-pleasing. I discovered that as an empath, we have an extreme love for people, are highly emotionally intuitive, and have a higher tolerance for abuse. Psychiatrist Judith Orloff (2017) indicated that trauma was the third reason why people become empaths. Notably, an empath is usually created by a narcissistic parent.

After giving birth to my daughter, I truly learned what love looks and feels like. I went on more of a self-discovery journey. I never wanted to hurt her like I was hurt. I wanted to know the causes of my own behaviors and of the behavior of those who hurt me. I discovered that one of the people who hurt me was a narcissist who was created during his childhood from abuse. And the other person was an empath, and she was also a product of narcissistic childhood abuse.

My Life-coach, Telsha Edenburgh (2021), indicated that "a narcissist and empath are born of the same house or same trauma." And guess what? I have always been drawn to narcissistic men.

GO FIGURE!

I was sexually abused and became a people pleaser and empath who buried her pain with achievements, but realized it was not enough and there was still a void. Case closed! No...Wrong again! If you dive a bit deeper into narcissism and the disorder associated with it, the spiritual association is connected to a very demonic force linked to the *Father of Lies or Satan*. These spirits wreck hell and havoc on the narcissist and empath's lives.

Now, do you see why I linked my own ***father*** with the *father of lies* in parity? This was not inadvertent parallelism on my part by any means. This was very intentional! You have to be an accursed, despicable and infernal individual to do something as unruly to your child or daughter, and I am confident many will agree. I digress once more.

Music is one of my most effective therapies; as a singer, songwriter, and pianist, you can speak freely, express yourself without judgment, and do it creatively. You can say what you want, how you want, and nobody cares because they are too busy vibin'[6] to the Music. The many songs about my life story, hurt, pain, and self-discovery were medicine to my soul. But this was still not enough to heal me but, only soothe me. It comforted me, but the healing still was incomplete and, unbeknownst to me, had not started.

The first step to healing is forgiveness, which was hard to get through. Being an empath, I can easily forgive others, but the challenge was forgiving myself. Again, I eventually forgave my ***father*** and mother, but I was still learning to forgive myself. I know you may be thinking that I did not do anything wrong. But hurt people… hurt people, and because I was hurt, I hurt others and then allowed others to hurt me again, and the cycle continued.

However, with God, goals, Music, and self-reflection led to individual therapy and life coaching. I was then able to process and start healing from the abuse, pain, neglect, abandonment, and internal torture. The Father of Lies no longer had me bound to these negative emotions and feelings. I told myself that these feelings were not of God and that this was NOT God's plan for me.

For I know the thoughts that I think toward you, saith the LORD, thoughts of peace, and not of evil, to give you an expected end. (Jeremiah 29:11, KJV)

My therapist, *Algernon Baker, Ph.D., LMFT,* and life coach *Telsha Edenburgh, BS, CPLC,* assisted me on a journey for the past two years to honestly know why specific things happened to me. And how I played a part in some things by allowing it, and how to change the trajectory to safeguard myself from specific issues not happening again. This is when I found true healing, and I am still pressing through. I am still here, standing, singing, writing, and talking to YOU! I discovered that my journey was all a part of the purpose-driven pain that unlocked a door and unleashed a beast that was buried in me. The unlocked door

---

[6] Slang of vernacular that means "to enjoy"

is for me to walk through and receive what God has for me, and the unleashed beast has left the building!

I never thought that I would have the ability not to allow my *father* to be a trigger. The sound of his voice would honestly send me back in time. Anyone healing from their past is on a journey within themselves. What allowed me to forgive my *father* was understanding.

Wisdom is the principal thing; therefore get wisdom: and with all thy getting get understanding (Proverbs 4:7, KJV)

I had to understand that he was abused, unloved, and abandoned as a child. His trauma caused the under-development of his psyche and produced multiple mental illnesses, which were later medically diagnosed. And he was a substance and drug user. Who can be in a proper state of mind with those levels of impairment? Finally, I have learned to understand that it was not me. It was him, and he would have to suffer the consequences of his actions. His life is still insatiable to this day. Not to say that his past justified his actions against me but know that God does not leave any diabolical acts unsettled.

My job was to now take care of Tiffany, forgive, heal and carry on.

I had to – I have to.

This is for the sake of my own creation and Young Queen, Journey Lindan Bell. Her life is predicated on my existence. So, I have to carry what my pain has guided me into my purpose. The purpose-driven pain has catapulted me to create Music, write songs, and even write this. The same pain that will assist me in going even further. Dr. Baker stated to "stop rehearsing yesterday and start remembering tomorrow" (2021).

Now, I am able to have entire conversations, go to lunch, and even do music performances with my Dad. Whether I tell him or not, I love my Dad for everything he is and everything he isn't. God did this as He sent his healing spirit and the right people and resources my way.

He is a Healer, *Jehovah Rapha,* and a Restorer, *Jehovah El-Ashiyb.*

I Praise Him and His son Jesus Christ for the Glory!

My angered temperament is not easily erupted, and I am no longer easily moved. Well…not as easy as it used to be.

I used to be a ticking time bomb awaiting detonation at the sight or sound of a threat. LOL.

Now, not so much!

I still have a way to go and some more healing to process, achieve and receive.

For now, this *God-fidence* that I have found is relieving as I am releasing!

I am a work in progress, yet a work of art!

– CrisTene

ABOUT THE AUTHOR

TIFFANY "CrisTene" WASHINGTON

Tiffany *"CrisTené"* Washington is a published author, singer-songwriter, and pianist. She was born and raised in Philadelphia, Pennsylvania.

Tiffany was a vocal music major while attending Philadelphia's Creative and Performing Arts High School (Jazmine Sullivan, Boys II Men, The Roots), where she was classically trained. She later graduated from Temple University with a Bachelor's in Music. Starting as an adolescent, Tiffany has been an active performer. As a result, Tiffany gains more confidence with each performance, or what she calls ***God-fidence***.

Tiffany completed her master's degree with a concentration in Public Health Administration. She further advanced her education by completing coursework for her second master's degree in education. Tiffany is currently a prospective law student.

Instagram: @cristene
https://www.instagram.com/cristene/

Facebook: cristenetriplet
https://www.facebook.com/cristenetriplet

TikTok: @cristenemusic
www.tiktok.com/@cristenemusic

YouTube: @cristenemusic
https://www.youtube.com/user/cristenemusic

Email: cristenemusic@gmail.com

CHAPTER TWELVE

Lopsided: Balancing the Scales of My Soul

BY DR. LATISHA WEBB

Have you ever felt lopsided? I mean, feeling completely empty on one side and weighed down on the other. Or, have you felt like an unbalanced scale that weighs down heavily on one side with your left leg and foot planted on the ground while your right leg and arm dangle in the air trying to find balance? This describes my thoughts and feelings while growing up without my daddy and paternal family. I felt as if my soul possessed unbalanced scales. Of course, I knew my mother and maternal family. I even knew my maternal grandfather and his family. However, I did not know my paternal side of the family, and my soul wandered around lopsided.

Let me share the backstory of my life. I was born and raised in Norfolk, Virginia. At the age of two, child protective services removed my three siblings and me from my mother's care. Thank God for loving maternal family members who huddled together to become kinship placements for us through legal proceedings in family court.

My mother's second eldest sister chose to raise me along with her husband and daughter. My aunt, uncle, and cousin became what I knew as *family*. Sheila, my cousin who helped raise me, loved my mother, whom she professed as her favorite aunt. Sheila told me many stories about my family, including stories about my daddy and paternal grandmother. As a matter of fact, Sheila taught me everything she knew. I learned about God, the birds and the bees, racism, and many other facts from Sheila. I soaked up Sheila's every word, especially when she shared with me about my parents. As I intently listened to Sheila, I envisioned my daddy as a tall, dark, handsome man with long coal-black wavy hair. Those stories turned the glimpses of my memories regarding my daddy from shades of gray to technicolor.

Two particular experiences colored my memory bank: (1.) the cadence of his voice when he called me Candy, his nickname for me; and (2.) the long way up, over 6 feet, from the floor to his bosom when he picked me up to hug and kiss me. I did not know much about my daddy's genetics. However, being the tallest girl in my class, I learned from Sheila when she jokingly said, *"you get your height from your daddy."* Sheila also told me that my *"long thick good hair that only needed water and grease"* came from my daddy.

Despite knowing that my height and hair texture came from my daddy, my soul remained lopsided in many ways because I missed out on many formulating experiences. I missed out on growing up in a two-parent household with my mother, daddy, and siblings living under one roof. I missed out on the primary social unit that most children need to thrive and understand who they are as individuals and members of a family, community, and society. This lopsidedness of my soul caused great psychological and emotional pain. For instance, I saw my mother and siblings on holidays and birthdays. Leaving them to return home to my aunt and uncle's house left me empty inside because I did not want the moment to end. However, not seeing my daddy and his family caused even more significant pain. I express gratitude for being a part of my maternal family, who allowed me to visit my mother and siblings without family court's intervention or supervision. Yet, I yearned for my daddy and his family. My eldest brother, James, and I share the same daddy. He is the closest relative that connected me to my daddy. But James and I traveled on the same boat. He equally struggled with not knowing and experiencing life with his paternal family. During some of James and my time together, certain maternal family members referred to us as *"Crawford's kids."*

James and I beamed whenever we heard it without knowing if we should feel insulted or complimented.

Although my maternal family refuses to refer to any siblings with different parents as half-brothers or half-sisters, James and I shared that special bond of having the same momma and daddy. We also shared a sense of pride as *Crawford's kids*, although we did not know what to be proud of. I expressed gratitude for this relationship with James, but my soul remained unbalanced. I yearned to know and experience my daddy and his family.

At the age of seven, God heard and responded to my soul's desire when my paternal aunt, Hattie, came to visit me. The one-day visit and short-lived experience that lasted a few hours left me with a faint memory and a wallet size picture of her that I kept in my beautiful white keepsake box. I remember staring at the picture of Aunt Hattie, trying to find some resemblance of me in her to bring soul balance. I did not find similarities between us because her skin complexion (lighter) and hair texture (shorter and relaxed) differed from mine. Having her picture generated new unanswered questions while leaving my soul even more lopsided. I treasured my beautiful white keepsake box adorned with blue and pink flowers and a small lock with a skeleton key. I kept all my nostalgic items dear to my heart in my beautiful white keepsake box, including two letters I received from my daddy during his time of incarceration. Oh my goodness, do I remember that beautiful white keepsake box that housed those letters and the wallet-size picture of Aunt Hattie.

Those two letters written by my daddy seemed huge to my seven-year-old self. The letters were on 11 by 14 legal size yellow lined paper and included beautifully hand-drawn colored flowers and calligraphic writing. Both letters began with my daddy referring to me as Candy, which I cherished for more reasons than one.

Not only did my daddy give me a nickname, but he also gave me my legal name, Latisha. Sheila shared with me that when my mother mentioned the name *"WaTina Demetria"* to my daddy, he said, "no, you are not naming my baby girl *WaTina Demetria*, after your best friend, Tina." Thank God for my daddy's intervention. Imagine growing up with the name WaTina! The thought of it makes me laugh out loud. When I read his two letters, everything from my nickname to the hand-drawn artwork to the style of writing to the ending words, "I love you," remained imprinted on my soul until this day. However, possessing those two letters left my soul even more lopsided because I wanted more. I desired a continuous, never-ending line of communication with my daddy through letter writing. I had so many unanswered questions. Again, I express gratitude for receiving those two letters; however, my soul remained lopsided and weighed down on the left side.

Many people referred to me as ungrateful while growing up. Externally, they saw the beautifully decorated home in the safe neighborhood with all Caucasian neighbors where my aunt and uncle raised me. They saw the latest clothes, a table filled with food three times/every day, and the luxury cars in the driveway. Yet, they did not see the intrinsic lopsidedness of missing both parents and never knowing my paternal family.

Another member of my maternal family who I hold dear to my heart includes my maternal grandmother, who raised the eldest of my four siblings, my only sister. I express gratitude for my relationship with my maternal grandmother, Grandma Lo, for taking my sister and me to Military Circle Mall, matinee movies at Janaf Shopping Center, and Piccadilly's Cafeteria in the summers. After church on Sundays, she took us to McDonald's for Hot Fudge Sundays with nuts and on rides to Waterside on the Trolley for just a quarter to catch a roundtrip ferry ride to Portsmouth, Virginia. I love my Grandma Lo. She brought so much joy to my life as a child.

Nevertheless, I express gratitude for the physical safety, morality, and stability provided by my aunt, uncle, and Sheila. I realize that some children cannot reminisce on any enjoyable moments. Even with all those loving members and memories of my maternal family, I remained lopsided and needed the soul balance of my daddy and his family.

I needed to know my daddy, aunts, uncles, and cousins. I needed to know what they liked, disliked, and shared interests. I just needed to know. Maybe the people in my life pegged me right when referring to me as ungrateful. I possessed so many blessings while equally lacking the basics. Being referred to as ungrateful by adults left my soul even more lopsided because no one around me cared to understand the unexpressed and unexplored depths of my soul living life without a daddy.

For example, the few, far, and in-between experiences with my daddy and his family remind me of a chocolate cupcake topped with buttercream frosting and covered with rainbow sprinkles. Imagine only picking off and enjoying the rainbow sprinkles and not indulging in the entire cupcake and buttercream frosting. The random experiences with my daddy and his family seemed like sprinkles that randomly landed on a cupcake. I wanted to indulge entirely and lick the spoon and bowl filled with left-over bittersweet chocolate batter. Like the chocolate cupcake topped with buttercream frosting and rainbow sprinkles, I wanted it all with my paternal family.

Without having it all, mommy, daddy, siblings, a home with us all living under one roof, visits in the summer down south to the Carolinas, family traditions, sitting on daddy's lap as his baby girl, having my brothers give my boyfriends the 'man talk,' looking up to my sister and getting beauty tips from her, having a favorite aunt and a first cousin as my best friend and without those Cosby-like sitcom-inspired, picture-perfect experiences, my soul felt lopsided. If that made me an ungrateful child at that time, today, being a mature adult, I own it and call myself ungrateful.

As a girl child, I needed a daddy to tell me about my beauty and value. I needed to learn how to handle the strength and power of a man's voice and tone. I needed my daddy to teach me about unacceptable interactions and non-negotiables in life and relationships. Simply put, I needed my daddy. I love my uncle for raising me. I understand that he *chose* to be in my life without blood relation. I appreciate him for that. Yet, I still needed my daddy. Without my daddy, my soul wandered around lopsided. Knowing that my height and hair texture came from my daddy brought a little balance, but it did not come close to what I needed. I stood tall, believing my daddy only fathered me and my brother James. Yet, I remained so unbalanced and lopsided that the scale of my soul tilted all the way down to the left. My soul rang with questions about my daddy and his family, such as, Who am I? Who are they? Do they love me? What are our commonalities? What do they think about me? Why didn't they come for me other than that one time when Aunt Hattie came to visit me?

Fast forward thirty-five years later, two of my paternal aunts *came* for me. One day I received a message on Facebook inquiring about my maiden name and if I had a brother named James? Although I was reluctant to respond, I received two more messages from Mary Bradford, who claimed to be my paternal aunt. Initially, I opened a Facebook account to promote my business, not to make personal connections. In lieu of *my* purpose for being on Facebook, God had His purpose, which included bringing more balance to my soul.

Accepting Jesus, the Christ, the Son of the Living God, as my personal Lord and Savior earlier in my life brought great healing and restoration to my soul. I learned that God, the Father, loved me, shaped me in my mother's womb, and chose to use my parents as the vessels to produce me. I learned that I belong to God, not man, and when my mother and daddy forsook me, God took me up. Consequently, I thought God balanced my soul in His healing and restoration as I finally walked upright in Him.

Unbeknownst to me, Father God, having my unbalanced soul in mind, wanted to make me whole. So, with ambivalence, I responded to that

Mary Bradford on Facebook after the fourth or fifth message with the subconscious thoughts, "I have a Daddy in God. I no longer need y'all as my family. I made it to grown womanhood without you." So, my written responses were short and sweet, including, "Greetings! Yes, my name is Latisha. And yes, I do have a brother named James."

Mary Bradford responded immediately with excitement leaping through the screen by saying, "Oh my God, here is my number. Please call me. I want to talk to you. My sister, Hattie, and I have looked for you for years. Please call me." With great apprehension, I called Mary Bradford. I remember hearing her voice for the first time. I instantly felt love emanating from the cell phone. I knew in my spirit that this woman loved me. I did not understand how a woman who had never met me, who I did not grow up with, who knew nothing about me, loved me. Yet, her love and genuineness touched the depths of my soul. During this initial call, Mary Bradford conferenced in her sister, Hattie, and I experienced a double whammy filled with the power of love, care, and concern. Then, it dawned on me. I remembered the wallet-size picture of my Aunt Hattie that I kept in my beautiful white keepsake box. Finally, after all those years, my Aunt Hattie and I conversed on the phone. God heard and responded to my soul's cry.

Aunts Mary and Hattie manifested as my paternal family members *who loved me, thought of me, and came looking for me.* God used the modern technology of Facebook to answer my prayers and to bring more balance to my soul. My relationship with my paternal family started with a message on Facebook, and we remained in communication after that. After three months of connecting and getting to know one another, Aunts Mary and Hattie traveled from North Carolina to Washington, DC, to watch me cross the stage with my doctoral degree. They gifted me with a framed 8.5 by 11 picture of my daddy in his high school cap and gown. I stared at that picture for what seemed like forever.

Looking back at me consisted of the 18-year-old man who fathered me. He looked very different than I remembered. His youth made me smile, and more questions flooded my soul. Instead of asking my aunts questions during the celebratory engagement, I simply hugged and thanked them. That gesture of kindness floored me. I experienced awe at being loved and supported by them in such a short period after meeting on Facebook. They expressed genuine happiness for finding me and my husband, Dr. William Webb, IV. Two years after my graduation, they visited us at our home in Philadelphia, Pennsylvania. My paternal aunts loved me, called me, visited me, prayed for me, and asked about every aspect of my life.

Plainly put, they loved me; thus, I loved them. I had never experienced that much genuine love before. I finally encountered what I missed growing up as a little girl without a daddy. Aunts Mary and Hattie told me stories about my paternal family, including my grandparents, aunts, uncles, and their children, and my first cousins on my daddy's side. In times of prayer and meditation, God revealed that He brought Aunts Mary and Hattie into my life for a more profound healing experience that only they possessed. Locked up in *their* souls consisted of *my* soul healing and gaining balance. Spending time conversing with them contained the keys that made my soul feel less lopsided.

Nine years after receiving that Facebook message, tragedy hit. Aunt Mary died from many health complications. In her death, she continued to fulfill her purpose of finding and bringing balance to my soul. I flew to Houston, Texas, for Aunt Mary's funeral. I had no agenda except to honor her life and her decision to look for and build a relationship with me. I wanted to meet my other paternal family members, but it came secondary to paying respect to one of two women who *came* for me and brought balance to my soul. I shared my gift of art and collage-making by creating a memoir of Aunt Mary. I left one with my family in Texas, and the other I brought back to Philadelphia. While sharing our first few family meals together at Aunt Mary's home in Houston, we observed one another, answered questions, and discussed facial features, voice tones, and body structures, to name a few.

We also discussed the family's plague: the incestual rape of my great-great-uncle, who raped his sister, my great-grandmother, and conceived a son, my grandfather. After my grandfather's birth, my great-grandmother left the Carolinas and relocated to Norfolk, Virginia, to reside with her sister and brother-in-law. My great-great-grandmother raised her grandson, my grandfather, who bore the shame of being the family's dark secret. After my daddy graduated from high school, he also moved to Norfolk, residing with his grandmother and other family members who relocated there before him.

Finally, for the first time, I felt my right foot on the ground and my right arm at my side no longer dangling in the air. I knew my daddy grew up in South Carolina, and my mother lived in Norfolk most of her life. Nevertheless, I did not know how their paths crossed. Then, alas, things became more apparent to me. Several paternal family members, including my daddy, fled their hometown in South Carolina for a better life in Norfolk. And then James, my daddy, met Annette, my mother.

As a child, I wondered if my parents truly loved one another. One story I remember my mother sharing about my daddy included me as "the love child." While in Texas, I learned from one of my uncles (Allen) that my daddy physically abused my mother. She kept that truth from me. However, I learned that my grandfather, the family's shameful secret, suffered greatly from rejection, ostracism, and abandonment. He missed out on love and acceptance from his mother, who fled to Norfolk, and his father, who did not embrace him. Instead, he transferred that soul hurt and harshness to his children, especially after his wife, my grandmother, died.

Flying back home to Philadelphia, Pennsylvania, from Houston, Texas, after the funeral with both of my feet firmly on the ground, I reconciled with my life. I now knew the other half of me. I express gratitude for God's divine providence for protecting and maturing me before learning the truth about the other half of my family's history. My childhood experiences made more sense as I reflected on the historical trauma that passed through my daddy's bloodline. God, the Father, finished His work of fully balancing, integrating, and giving me access to my paternal family. I am forever grateful to Aunt Mary for her life and to Aunt Hattie, whom I love dearly. I am grateful to my first cousin Lin, his wife and family, and other paternal family members for remaining in contact with me after Aunt Mary's funeral. They welcomed and called me one of their own. They keep the scales of my soul balanced.

Dr. Latisha Webb

ABOUT THE AUTHOR

DR. LATISHA WEBB

Although I grew up without my daddy and experienced the grief from his death from AIDS-related complications before my 15th birthday, he blessed me with the gift of introspection, empathy for those who are incarcerated, the power of letter writing, and art. Each of these gifts' manifests in my life today. My daddy's absence, incarceration, and death intertwine with my purpose in six great ways:

1. Missing my natural daddy drove me to my knees, where I met my Heavenly Daddy, Father God. Desperate for love and acceptance, God saved, healed, delivered, and adopted me as His own. As a disciple of Jesus Christ, I learned about spiritual gifts and callings. I accepted my call and serve as a Pastor in the Lord's church.

2. As an introverted woman who prays and meditates, I embrace the solitude thrust upon me during my childhood (growing up) without my mother, daddy, and siblings. Experiencing that solitude enables me to continuously ask deep questions about the purpose of my existence. I seek Authenticity in all six

dimensions, spiritual, psychological, emotional, sexual, physical, and social, through my brand, Advancing Authenticity. I also author various types of topical journals titled *I am Grateful: Manifesting Gratitude, You are Be-YOU-Tiful Personal Notebook, Prayer for Journal for Women,* and *The Self-Care for Black Women,* sold only on Amazon.

3. Asking profound questions created a space for me to pursue higher levels of education and conduct research. Advancing Authenticity derived from my dissertation research, *Discovering the Authentic Self: The Concurrent Processes of Being and Becoming.* Having a doctorate opened doors for me as an adjunct professor who teaches adult learners pursuing their associate's and bachelor's degrees.

4. In pursuit of my life's purpose, God allowed a purpose-driven man to find me. My husband, Dr. William Webb, IV. His heart beats for serving the community, including those incarcerated, by impacting their lives. As co-founders of Opportunity, Inc., a nonprofit organization based in Philadelphia, Pennsylvania, we create, connect and advance others through communal art projects and training and development programs for formerly and currently incarcerated individuals.

5. Those two letters I received from my daddy during his incarceration, with the hand-drawn artwork and calligraphic writing, exuded power that exploded later in my life. As a self-taught abstract multimedia creative, I create art for all types of community connections. One of Opportunity, Inc.'s programs, Sista2Sista Soul2Soul, includes facilitating communal art projects with women on the outside and turning the finished artwork into greeting/postcards sent to women on the inside. With volunteers across the United States, we use the branded greeting cards to write letters to over 300 women serving 20 or more years in Pennsylvania's penal institutions.

6. Creating art for community connections crosses over into creating coloring books titled, *Dimensions of Art Coloring Book for Self Care and Relaxation,* also only sold on Amazon. Filled

with pages of original artwork from my personal collections, I use a cartoon filter for texture and a black and white filter for clarity to make the coloring pages. Now, I help others engage in self-care and relaxation activities while enjoying their "me moments" of solitude.

To learn more about my products and services, go to www.flow.page/drlatishawebb/

To follow me on Instagram, search @drlatishawebb

To learn more about Opportunity, Inc.'s programs, go to www.opportunitytoadvance.com

To follow Opportunity, Inc. on Instagram, search @opportunity2advance

CHAPTER THIRTEEN

Shaken But Not Stirred

BY CAPATORIA WILSON

For as long as I can remember, I've always LOVED James Bond. The very first actor portraying James Bond, 007, that I can remember is Sean Connery in "Dr. No" 1962. So, of course, we all remember him as the first Bond, right? WRONG! But, as memorable as he was with his British accent, sports cars, guns blazing, a fantastic soundtrack, he was not her Majesty the Queen's first 007.

James Bond began in unofficial films, T.V. series, and radio shows, dating back to 1954 with Barry Nelson, according to the article "Who Played James Bond: A Complete History." We find him rushing to assist "MI-6," a Secret Intelligence Service headed by "M" of British Intelligence. "M" commands and James Bond responds to foil diabolical deeds as Ian Fleming's masterpiece unveils itself in theaters and on television screens worldwide.

Women have a way of swooning over James Bond, who coins a memorable phrase that follows him in most movies "Shaken, not stirred," referring to his signature drink, "Martini and vodka on the rocks. The phrase that suggests, with a slight alteration, the first time I remember meeting my father, hence "SHAKING, NOT STIRRED."

I don't remember the day or the hour. I can't remember whether the moon was shining at night or if it was a bright sunny day. I cannot remember much, but I do remember running into a closet, hiding while the hanging clothes became my shield and fortress of protection, defending me from what I was about to face. I kneeled in the closet that day, shaking like a leaf on the tree on an extremely windy day.

It was the day I was told that my father was coming over. I was less than six years old at the time. I don't remember meeting him. I don't remember coming out of the closet that day, but I must have. I only remember being afraid and shaking in that courtyard apartment building on Stoney Island.

My older cousin says she remembers that day very well and vividly recalls what happened. She recounts that I seemed to have thought that my father was going to take me away from the safety of the only life I'd known, our grandmother, brother, and three cousins. Hence, I hid in the closet, scared and shaking. My cousin remembers my brother, our grandfather, grandmother, and herself in the apartment. She says my brother was aloof and eventually walked away as our grandparents sat at the table talking with my father. My brother went somewhere else in our oversized apartment, with a very long hallway in a courtyard building on Stony Island, but I ran and hid in my citadel, the closet. She further relayed that she stayed there listening, interested, talking, and, I'm sure, asking more questions as I remained incognito. She remembers me coming out of the closet after he left and my Father/ Daughter chronicle began.

That early story of my life would later sum up my interactions with most men from that day forward, except my grandfather and uncles, who were always around.

I came to FEAR every time I attended meetings with men in authority. I continued to ask, "what did I do wrong?" Something was missing from my life. I suffered from my perceived rejection, and I was never good enough. I was seeking the approval of a father figure that I'd not known or had in my younger years. This thought process would cost me over and over again. James Bond's phrase, "Shaken but not stirred," was my reality. I was still in that closet, shaking at the thought of seeing my father for the first time I could remember. I was walking through life shaking at every opportunity or encounter with men, and no one stirred, jostled, or addressed my fear! How could they? I never uttered a word about it until recently.

We later moved to the projects, where I grew up in the "Ickes" public housing complex." Not many fathers were around during this era. The complex expanded about three blocks and contained about sixteen buildings with seven to nine floors each. There were an awful lot of apartments encompassing a whole lot of fatherless families. Fathers were a minority, and a sighting of one was a treat for all of us, well, at least for me, anyway.

I remember almost every time my oldest friend in the world's father visited her. She beamed with excitement, just knowing her father was coming. It was a fantastic feeling for her but also a treat for me as she recounted the hours spent with her dad. I missed that part of growing up. I longed for it, I ached for it, and I COVERED IT UP! I wore a mask for years as if it didn't matter. Although I pretended that it wasn't necessary, my actions, desires, and life's quest always displayed a craving for that wish to be fulfilled.

I sought approval and acceptance from men and allowed my heart to be vulnerable because I thought I needed the validation of a man to feel important. I could've saved myself countless hours, days, and years of disappointments, sleepless nights, and innumerable heartaches while settling for less than I deserved. If only I'd understood that I was looking for love in all the wrong places.

It was God, the Father's love, that I wanted and needed. The creator of all humanity, a true Father's love. How could I trust God? He, too, was always portrayed as a man. In my experience, as well as multiple families in the Ickes, we all understood that "FATHERS WERE NEVER PRESENT." I was doomed! It took me several years to unpack and process that untruth, but to me, it was real.

I saw this from a child's perspective and internalized it as a child. I did not "put away childish things when I grew older." Not knowing my father in my early years would rule my choices in my life, and I would continue searching for a "Father's Love." If only I'd known that all I had to do was look inside myself for the answer hidden in my heart which reminds me of the scripture, *Proverbs 25:2 – "It is the glory of God to conceal a matter and the honor of kings to search it out."* I did not know the answer was inside of me!

However, I do know that each time I came close to being judged, asked to explain, or entering a relationship with a man, my reality was, "you're not worthy; HE'S GONNA LEAVE YOU," and I had to unpack that lie that ruled my life for years.

Rejection was an actual occurrence in my life. I was raised by my grandmother, whose mother died at a young age, who sent her daughter (my mother) to live with her aunt (for medical purposes) at a young age. My father's mother (I later learned) passed away at an early age, leaving his aunt to raise him as an only child, is what I believe.

There were not many men around me growing up, except my auntie's husbands and my grandfather, who showed up every weekend. They did not know that I was "SHAKING and NOT STIRRED" inside.

It was stated that James Bond requested alcoholic beverages shaken because he drank a lot. His catchphrase, "Shaken, Not Stirred," possibly resulted from his inability to stir drinks which led to an alcohol-induced tremor affecting his hands." So, as outlined in the article, "Why James Bond Wanted Martinis' Shaken Not Stirred,' by Bahar Gholipour. According to the article and after copiously studying Bond films for hours, Bond drank like an alcoholic, Ms. Gholipour concluded. Indeed, he was masking something like me, maybe even you, right?

We later learn that Bond was an orphan. He had neither of his parents. Maybe that's why so many of us love Mr. Bond so much.

He had a hard life, something we can relate to in one way or another. Neither of us handled life's stresses very well, and both of us numbed our pain and found a way to "FIGHT OUR WAY THROUGH IT." Maybe you can insert yourself into the story of "Having a difficult life too."

When I think of James Bond, I think of my father, whose mother died when he was two. He was left to be raised by an auntie. My father's father was a military career infantry soldier and later joined the national guards. His time in the military apparently diminished father and son quality time. Although my father expressed that his dad visited him at every opportunity, the lack of visits hurt. My granddad introduced my dad to his wife and other siblings.

I wonder what kind of impact missing quality time with his dad may have had on my dad in his younger years. Furthermore, I wonder how that impact shaped my dad's idea of fatherhood. I am delighted that my dad later remarried and raised my other siblings (a brother and sister), for which I am thankful. However, I am sorry that the brother I grew up with and I, for whatever reason, were not able to know our father earlier in life, which I believe was a repetitive cycle affecting both generations (more thoughts on this later).

James Bond's face changed as different actors portrayed his character. In a 1967 James Bond spoof, "Casino Royale," David Niven plays retired 007, who returns to action after his home is blown up. "M" is killed, and James Bond comes out of retirement to take control of MI-6 and names every secret service agent "007 or James Bond" to confuse and foil the enemy's sinister plan.

Like Bond, naming every MI-6 agent "James Bond," there were quite a few men with different names and personalities representing a "father." Each poured into me the best of who they were by foiling the enemy's plan over my life and making me better due to their input. Although I didn't meet my father until my late 20', I was blessed to have "Father figures" in my life while growing up who loved and treasured me as their own child, which I think gave me some semblance of security.

James Bond had "M," which is more of an office (Mission) than a name, "M" represented stability in James Bond's life as "father" represented figureheads in my life growing up. So likewise, today, I am a compilation of the many fathers that poured into my life and helped me become the person I am now.

The good, the bad, and the ugly seasons of life help us become who we are today. It may not have been the easiest road, but every aspect of your journey represents who you are currently. I do not deny the power of my grandmother, grandfather, mother, aunties, uncles, brother, cousins, and family, for they are the real heroes of my story. I thank God and them for their daily input in my life, and watching over me is why I am me. Special kudos go to my brother, who stood up for me more times than I can count. He wasn't my father, but he also did some fathering to me in some ways.

Bond was portrayed by different faces, for different seasons, at different times, and for different purposes. My life was similar to Bond in that respect. And men were in and out of my life for the same reasons.

One such man was my cousin's father, Uncle Charles. I remember (ever so clearly) riding on Lake Shore Drive with the breeze from the lake blowing through the window and looking at the beautiful boats on the water. This was one of my favorite times as a youngster. My aunt, Tee Tee, and her husband, Uncle Charles, usually took us out for a ride, I don't remember the car, but it had to be pretty big to fit all five kids into it.

I loved my aunts. They were married, and seeing them as a child was exciting. Both husbands were coincidentally named Charles. But Uncle Charles, Tee Tee's husband, would always take us places, and they took us together, as husband and wife. It was good seeing a father coming around our family of five children. My cousins and I share many laughs about the times we spent together.

My uncle Charles and my Aunt Tee Tee took us to amusement parks, car rides on Lake Shore Drive, and trips to see Christmas decorations. With windows down – fresh air blowing in the car while going to auto shows at McCormick Place. We had to travel down Lake Shore Drive to get there. We went fishing at the lagoon, close to the 63rd street beach. The skyscrapers, the lights shining brightly at night, oh, the peace I felt in the back seat of that car (when we weren't arguing). Can you tell me which was my favorite time? If you've never seen it, YEP, Lake Shore Drive is a "must-see." If you have seen it, you understand.

My uncle Charles came into our lives to raise his daughters with his wife, but for me, it was to help me see men and a father's love. His love extended to those of us whose father wasn't present. He helped me see unconditional love from a man for the first time.

My mother dated as I grew older, and they also became great father figures. I was blessed to have her choose men that thought of me as their daughter and treated me that way. Like James Bond changed actors throughout history, I had different men (in my life) represent a father's love at various stages of life. I thank God for the different faces that stood in the gap as I grew up. Although their names were different, love was nearby.

As I reached high school age, I wondered what my father looked like, where he lived, if I'd ever meet him, or if I'd met him already. I could've passed him on the street and never knew who he was. I had a picture, but I didn't know him. I didn't know the sound of his voice. I knew he sang, so I figured he had to have a decent voice. Questions I asked myself were, "What was he like? Where were my grandparents? Did I have any additional sisters or brothers? The questions kept coming, but I had no answers. Finally, I realized I might never know these answers, and I had to be content with that fact.

As I sit here telling my story, I am looking at a cup that says, "Choose to Find Joy," something we all must do in life. Although the answers you desire may not come as you'd please, we've got to see the rainbow in the clouds, the sunshine after the rain, and the rainfall making the flowers grow. In other words, "Whatever state you find yourself in, BE CONTENT, for sometimes that's the best you can get.

Another James Bond character is "Q," who showed up when 007 needed equipment. There have been approximately six men who have played that role throughout the James Bond movies. "Q" stands for Quartermaster. It is not a name. Instead, it is a job title in which he heads the "Q-Branch or the research and development division of the British Secret Service. "Q" continues to develop exploding pens, fire-bombing cars, listening devices, and special equipment for James Bond. Looking at our past lives, we will see that different people were assigned to help us become equipped to be our best selves.

It is a blessing to see fathers raising their children, but the reality is that many fathers were not raised by their fathers nor had fatherly input in their lives. If we, as people, are products of our environment, unless fathers of today take time to learn how to become fathers, they will operate at a deficit. We can no more expect a duck to behave like a cat than a child raised without strong fatherly input.

I applaud my brother, with whom we were raised together. He understood the pain of not having a father in his life to guide him along his life's journey, so he made sure to raise his own children together with his wife.

I thank my husband, who grew up with a father. He understood that I purposely engaged in behavior and ran him away so he wouldn't hurt me by leaving. He assured me he wasn't going anywhere and never did.

I thank my father-in-love, who displayed unconditional love toward me from the time I became involved in a relationship with his son. He embraced me totally as I celebrated my strengths without hesitation or reservations.

I thank my grandfather for always being there for me. While growing up, we sat and talked about everything with love in his heart.

I thank the male police officers that worked with me and made me feel that I was somebody to know.

I thank the male ministers who celebrated God's anointing on my life and helped me become the best I could be.

I thank the many men who have helped me grow and develop into a woman who adds value to the world and the lives of others.

I thank my father, who did his best to be his best while working out his problems and is still with us today.

I am thankful for "YOU," the natural, stand-in, and spiritual fathers who are standing in the gap for children and helping them have better lives today.

We are people with broken parts, and blaming everyone else will only exacerbate our lives further. Instead, let's look at each other through the lens of love, the one and only Wise God, who is Father to the fatherless and mother to the motherless. The one we gather wisdom and knowledge from and release that to others who may not be able to process it. Let's pray for our fathers and men and build them up instead of tearing them down.

I speak life over the fathers and young men who have trouble becoming their best selves. I talk about love and healing over families that have been beaten down and broken down at the hand of fatherlessness or a furiously frustrated father.

I speak and seek protection and correction to a faulty system that promoted removing fathers from communities that may have had a hand in encouraging fathers to leave home.

I speak abundant life to broken families with broken hearts, dreams, and lives that suffered due to a lack of a father's touch or a response to an angry father's touch.

I speak life, wisdom, understanding, and love to the broken, shattered hopes and dreams of unfulfilled expectations from fatherlessness.

I speak a direction change and abundant life to those fathers on street corners hustling and those in prison hurting.

Let us feel and imitate the love of God as a Father who never leaves nor forsakes us. Help us tap into God's love so strongly that it helps us recover all we've lost over our lifespan.

Lord, help us learn how to embrace fathers and love them back into their rightful positions so that our neighborhoods prosper as God intended.

Lord God, let our men reclaim their rightful places as leaders so that we may pursue our destined places of victory together as God's great army. May we overtake and eradicate the pain and scars that have kept us separated and bound. Teach us to continue pressing forward without failing and recover all God intended for us to possess.

Thank You, Father, for restoring hope. Thank you for healing the hurts of disjointed families and helping us forgive one another as we rebuild our lives together as one big GODLY FAMILY THROUGHOUT THE WORLD, in Jesus' Name.

> *"I'll hazard I can do more damage on my laptop, sitting in my pajamas before my first cup of Earl Grey than you can do in a year in the field."*
> — Q, to James Bond[src]

Q (stands for Quartermaster), like <u>M</u>, is a job title rather than a name. He is the head of the <u>Q Branch</u>, the fictional research and development division of the <u>British Secret Service</u>.

Life as well. 2 Peter 3:1-3

Capatoria Wilson, AKA Pastor Tori, PT

ABOUT THE AUTHOR

**CAPATORIA WILSON
AKA PASTOR TORY, PT**

Pastor Tory would rather be known as God's humble servant, his child, and loves wearing her tee-shirt, saying, "I don't know about you, but I am GOD'S FAVORITE." Tory spent twenty-five years working for the police department, where she met the man she would marry, and together they raised four children. She was also blessed to have five beautiful grandchildren whom she loves dearly. She is a retired widow, daughter, sister, loving mother of four, and proud grandmother of five.

As a precocious child, she became a versatile and formidable ambassador for Christ and a faithful friend to many. Tory came from humble beginnings, raised by her grandmother while her mother worked. She grew up in the projects with her brother, three cousins, and many kids who didn't know their fathers. Although they didn't have much, they always had great meals to eat, clean clothes to wear, and a warm bed to sleep in. In addition, her grandmother made sure they went to Sunday School on Sunday morning and service afterward. This was the setup for her calling in the life of ministry.

Tory has traveled to thirty of our fifty states, and she is a Certified John Maxwell Trainer. In addition, she is a graduate and certified speaker with Inspired2Speak (Dr. James Dentley). Tory has a plethora of certifications. Marriage and family counseling is the ministry of her heart. She currently cares for her mother. She is a wellness coach, an avid reader, and loves teaching and studying God's word. She is a Life Changer- a Health and Wellness Coach with Total Life Changes- offering all-natural supplements for a healthier you.

She is the author of "When The Rain Falls the Flower Blooms: Surviving difficult times in marriage and relationships." You will find her planting seeds of hope for family healing, wealth, and health. She is honored and grateful to be a part of this project, and hopefully, something said will bless the lives of others.

Above all, it is all about winning souls for Christ for Pastor Tory. It has been about winning souls and healing the hearts of God's people. She has a charge to keep giving and gives 135% to it.

Many scriptures touch Pastor Tory, but none so much as I Sam 30:18 KJV.

1 Samuel 30:8 KJV – And David enquired at the LORD, saying, Shall I pursue after this troop? Shall I overtake them? And he answered him, Pursue: for thou shalt surely overtake them, and without fail recover all.

1 Samuel 30:*18 KJV – And David recovered all that the Amalekites had carried away: and David rescued his two wives.*

1 Samuel 30:19 KJV – And there was nothing lacking to them, neither small nor great, neither sons nor daughters, neither spoil nor anything that they had taken to them: David recovered all,

AND, LIKE DAVID, THAT IS WHAT PASTOR TORY INTENDS TO DO!

REFERENCES/TIFFANY WASHINGTON

Floyd, J. (2021). *GodFidence*. William Commerce.

English Standard Version. (2001) https://www.biblegateway.com/

The Holy Bible, King Version (2016). Thomas Nelson.

New International Version. (2011) https://www.biblegateway.com/

Standhart, M. (2021, June 11). *The Downside of People Pleasing*. Family Counselor, I Westminster, CO. Retrieved February 16, 2022, from https://www.themarriageandfamilyclinic.com/make-the-most-of-the-season-by-following-these-simple-guidelines

Cloud, H., & Townsend, J. (1992). *Boundaries: When to say yes, when to say no to take control of Your life*. Zondervan.

Orloff, J. (2017, June 22). Four Reasons Why People Become Empaths: Trauma to Genetics. *Psychology Today*. Retrieved February 16, 2022, from https://www.psychologytoday.com/us/blog/the-empaths-survival-guide/201706/four-reasons-why-people-become-empaths-trauma-genetics